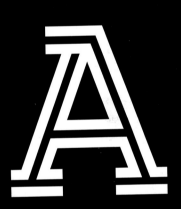

Contents

Introduction

By Brendan Quinn

One does not sit down, start pounding keys and expect to encompass the meaning of a championship in the annals of Kansas basketball. You don't simply take on something so large. Perhaps John McPhee could do it. He once spent 20 years writing a 700-page book explaining how North America was formed. Maybe that's what it takes.

Such a vast, scaling history is something Bill Self spent so much of the past two decades trying to get his arms around.

The Kansas coach is, in fact, a native Oklahoman who, upon landing the KU job in 2003, had no prior connections to the school other than a single season as a graduate assistant under Larry Brown in the mid-1980s. Self was, nevertheless, given the seat at the right hand of the father for a program founded by Dr. James Naismith, the man who invented the sport. Things started smashingly. Self won a national title in Year 5 and rolled along, averaging over 30 wins a year, cementing his 2017 induction into the Hall of Fame in Springfield, Mass. — the one named after Naismith.

But of late, in a sport measured most by the first Monday night in April, Kansas existed as a program desperate to resolve its contradictions. Yes, KU is college basketball's all-time winningest program. And yes, it plays in the game's greatest gym. But blue-blood brothers Duke and North Carolina have both won two national championships apiece since Kansas' last title in 2008. So have Villanova and Connecticut, ephemeral blue bloods. Hell, even Baylor, an old Big 12 doormat back in the day, has won a title more recently than Kansas.

Meanwhile, there was Self, holding on to his one title like a wilted flower.

"We've had some really terrific seasons and some great teams that came up short," he said not too long ago. "At most places, winning one national championship would be quite an accomplishment. But I do think, as many good teams as we've had, one's not enough."

That changed, at last, on April 4, 2022 in New Orleans. In its 50th NCAA Tournament, its 16th Final Four and its 10th national championship game, Kansas won its fourth national title in school history. The Jayhawks did it with a team that might not rank as one of Self's best teams, talent-wise. It was, instead, a championship run based on resilience and experience.

They went down in order: Texas Southern and Creighton in rounds one and two. Providence and Miami in the Sweet 16 and Elite Eight. Then a trip to the Superdome. A blue-blood Final Four of Kansas, Villanova, Duke and North Carolina amounted to mutually assured destruction for all, except one survivor.

In the semifinals, KU knocked off short-handed Villanova. Then North Carolina ended Mike Krzyzewski's reign with an upset for the ages.

It was Kansas-North Carolina in the finals, a game with all the fixings. The programs are entwined in history. There's Dean Smith, a KU grad with a Hall of Fame tenure at UNC. There's Roy Williams, a UNC grad who coached KU to four Final Fours before heading home to replace Smith at UNC in 2003, creating the opening that led to Self.

Kansas won, thanks to the remnants of a team that could've very well won a 2020 title had a pandemic not changed the world. This team's two senior leaders were toss-ins in Self's 2018 recruiting class, one headlined by five-stars Quentin Grimes and Devon Dotson.

Ochai Agbaji, the tournament's Most Outstanding Player, was ranked outside the top 300 among 2018 recruits when Self offered him a scholarship. David McCormack had size and was highly ranked but also a bit of a project. By the end of 2022, Agbaji was a national player of the year candidate and McCormack went from pensive post player to fire-snorting big man. Meanwhile, second-leading scorer Christian Braun was a former three-star recruit, rangy wing Jalen Wilson was picked up after a decommitment from Michigan and Remy Martin was fished out of the transfer portal.

It felt appropriate. For years, Kansas waded in the waters of sexy recruits and one-and-dones. It produced a lot of wins, a lot of Big 12 championships. But annually, come April, the Jayhawks were already out the door, looking for their home in the NBA.

This group? It came back. And it played in April. Maybe Martin, a transfer from Arizona State, said it best: "If you're at Kansas, you're meant to be at Kansas. Once you know you belong, it all takes care of itself. You feel the weight, you understand the weight, but you also feel comfortable carrying the weight."

Even if it's heavy. Even too heavy.

Just ask Self. In late January, two days before a game at Kansas State, his father, Bill Sr., died at the age of 82. The loss, of course, knocked Self off his moorings. But he worked through it, deciding not to skip the game at K-State.

The Jayhawks found themselves down by 16 at the half. Then, a massive rally. A team playing for its coach. A game-winning scoop shot by Agbaji stole a victory for KU. The postgame locker room was a scene. Self came in running, glasses on the bridge of his nose, jumping into his guys' arms. After the celebration, he smiled, looked up and said, "You guys know this," before swallowing a massive lump in his throat, pausing and finishing. "This one means something."

It did. And so did the next one. When Kansas returned home for a game against Texas Tech, some KU students hung a banner on the front row of the baseline. It read: "JUST LOAD THE WAGON."

See, Bill Sr. had this saying. He repeated it to Bill Jr. for years. It was a reminder that you can only control what you can control, that intent is more important than outcome.

"Don't worry about the mules," Bill Sr. would say. "Just load the wagon."

Sometimes, that's enough to get you where you're trying to go.

For the 2022 Jayhawks, it got them to a place in history. ▬▬

NCAA Tournament Final Four

```
SCORING      1   2   T
Villanova   29  36  65
Kansas      40  41  81
```

All Is Well

David McCormack Leads Kansas into the National Title Game

By CJ Moore

APRIL 2, 2022

David McCormack was two seats down from Bill Self on the dais. His head was cocked forward, listening along as his coach spoke, saying that familiar word, once again. Frustrated. It's long been the knock on McCormack. So good, but so frustrating. As Self said it, a big grin formed on McCormack's face.

McCormack has heard about it plenty, getting the quick hook when he missed bunnies or put the ball on the floor when he shouldn't or didn't grab a rebound or simply didn't play to his size. As soon as it happens, it's like a built-in reflex for Self, immediately turning to his bench and signaling for Mitch Lightfoot to enter the game.

McCormack, the young man, is easy to love. He graduated from Kansas in three years. He's introspective, sometimes overthinking the game and letting little hiccups stay in the memory bank, leading to more misses. He's a mama's boy. "And he's not afraid to say it," Janine McCormack says, a big smile on her face after watching her baby play the game of his life. They talk every day. Never about basketball. It's his moment each day to simply escape from those pressures. They end every conversation telling each other, "All is well."

And even in his worst moments when he's gone to the bench after a mistake, McCormack encourages. Never pouts. Simply moves on to the next thing.

All is well.

8

All has not been well exactly, his mom knows, when it comes to his right foot. He hurt it during the first round of the 2021 NCAA Tournament, then had surgery on it almost exactly a year ago. That thing screams at him sometimes. Sometimes he looks old. Sometimes it looks like it's hard to move. Hell, it hurts just to watch him move.

But McCormack, even on his worst days, found ways to be effective anyway, becoming one of the country's best offensive rebounders and getting really good at drawing fouls. McCormack has been a good college big man these last two years. He was KU's star during the second half of 2020-21. His greatest sin, simply, is that he followed Udoka Azubuike, the prototypical big in Self's system.

You could not move Azubuike. He scored off angles. His hands became vise grips. He scored above the rim, dunking with power any time he got within reach of it. Defensively, the paint was like quicksand for anyone who dared to challenge Azubuike at the basket, and during his senior season when he got in the greatest shape of his life, he could slide his feet on the perimeter too. His defense basically made ball-screen offense a non-factor.

It's why two years ago, Kansas may have shredded the bracket had there been one, because no one had a player like Azubuike and no one could stop him.

It was easy to think this season, when Ochai Agbaji became an All-American and KU had the best wing trio in the country and eventually a flamethrower off the bench in Remy Martin, *what if* Kansas had an Azubuike in there with them?

For one night, at least, no one on the Kansas bench was thinking that. Because they saw it.

David McCormack was that dude.

Jay Wright left his press conference after experiencing a clinical onslaught from Kansas in its 81-65 victory, and he saw a familiar face in the hallway of the Caesars Superdome. It was Big East commissioner Val Ackerman. "They shoot like that, man," he told Ackerman, pausing for a second for emphasis. "Whew."

Wright was much like Self four years ago on this Final Four stage, helpless and hopeless.

"They started making jumpers," he said, "and we were spread out."

Wright will go to sleep, much like Self had done in 2018, knowing there was really nothing he could do. Agbaji ruined his game plan by banging four 3s early — he'd go on to make his first six — and it put Villanova's defense in a bind. Stick with Agbaji? Or with McCormack?

The Wildcats made the logical move, trying to cheat off others, like Dajuan Harris, but even he made three treys. The confidence transferred from Agbaji and McCormack to everyone else.

Thing is, just about no one does this to Villanova. You have to go back to 2017 to find a higher efficiency mark against the Wildcats. This one was sixth-best ever against Wright's defense, according to KenPom.com's numbers. It was the second-best mark KU put up all season — the Missouri game could not be topped — but considering the stage and the defense, let's go ahead and get hyperbolic: This was one of the best offensive performances in Kansas history. Eighty-one points in 58 possessions without a transition bucket? Ridiculous.

Right up there with Danny Manning and the Miracles at Kemper Arena in 1988 when they decided to run with Oklahoma. Right up there with Kansas against North Carolina in 2008.

The Jayhawks, in many ways, out-Nova'd Nova. They shot-faked on long closeouts. They made extra passes. And they buried 13 3s.

Those shots were made so easy because of McCormack. Even when Agbaji and McCormack weren't scoring, their gravity opened up the floor for everyone else.

"He was outstanding," Wright said. "It's not just him being outstanding, it's their execution and their schemes to get him the ball at the right spots."

Others had tried that in this tournament. Michigan, in particular. But most teams cannot get the ball to those spots or finish over Villanova. Eventually, bigs just wear out from the Wildcats leaning on you for 40 minutes. Michigan's Hunter Dickinson can attest.

McCormack knew what was coming. Kansas assistant and big-man whisperer Norm Roberts gave him the scouting report. "He told me they like to wall up and chest into you," McCormack said. "They collapse down on the dribble, so you just have to go straight up and get right into your shot."

McCormack was quick into his moves, scoring on jump hooks over both shoulders with both hands, and finishing through contact. He scored a career-high 25 points on 10-of-12 shooting.

"I've said all along he's the one guy on our team who can get 15 and 10 just by being a presence," Self said. "Tonight he got 25 and nine. He was fabulous."

To simply focus on his offense, however, would not do justice to the complete performance he had. Remember four years ago. Kansas struggled to guard a Villanova lineup featuring a stretch five. Azubuike had no interest in defending the perimeter.

McCormack, ailing foot and all, hasn't always thrived guarding on the perimeter, either. But on this night he slid his feet, staying in front of Villanova's wings and allowing KU to stay sound off the ball. The Wildcats were at their best when McCormack went to the bench, so they could crash the glass and get kick-out 3s. But with him in the game, Kansas outscored Villanova by 25.

This was McCormack's best game ever, on both ends.

"By far," assistant coach Jeremy Case said.

Once McCormack was finished putting his team in the national championship game, he took a seat on the bench, pounded his chest once, kissed his fist and then pointed to the sky.

Afterward, he said that his foot is just fine. "I'm on a complete adrenaline high," he said. "Feeling great."

All is well.

———————— ————————

Janine, who lives in Virginia, estimates this night was only the 12th time in 129 times her son has played for Kansas that she's been able to be there in person. She often watched from a distance.

It's hard for a mom to be that far away, especially when her boy hurts. She prayed that God would give her son the strength to have his moment.

"He's got strength," she said. "You know God gave him strength."

That strength made it so Villanova had no answer on this night. The Wildcats could not move McCormack. They couldn't do anything with him. Janine couldn't pick a favorite moment because there were so many.

Janine had one more point she wanted to get across. This night was spectacular. It was sweet. It's been a journey. The ups and downs. But there's still one more game to go, and she's not ready to say this was the best he'll ever be.

"The championship game," she said, "is going to be the pinnacle." ▬▬

NCAA Tournament Championship

```
SCORING            1   2   T
North Carolina    40  29  69
Kansas            25  47  72
```

Unprecedented

No. 1 Kansas Overcomes 15-Point Halftime Deficit to Win National Championship

By CJ Moore

APRIL 4, 2022

After he'd cut down the net following his second national title, Bill Self called for center David McCormack and met him at the top of the key. Self put his right arm around McCormack's neck and pulled him in close, whispering in his ear, "Ochai (Agbaji) got the hardware, but you get the net."

Self took the freshly-cut net in his left hand and put it right into McCormack's chest. The big fella, who always had the belief of his coach even if some questioned it, had come through for Kansas on the biggest stage, scoring the final four points of the greatest comeback in championship game history.

"All year in the most clutch times, times when the game is on the line, he put the ball in my hands," McCormack, the net now draped around his neck, said. "It shows that he loves me. He feels that I deserved that and that I worked hard to get in this position."

Faith can do miraculous things, and Self found himself looking upward a lot the last few months.

A day after his father's death in January, Self's team trailed by 16 at rival Kansas State. Self told himself that day that he'd stay calm and wouldn't blow up on his guys. It was a lesson Bill Sr. taught him long ago. *Don't blow up about the big things.* They rewarded him with a win. In the Elite Eight when they'd played tight against Miami and trailed by six at half, Self was stern but calm, giving his team the blueprint for a comeback. A mantra the Jayhawks adopted late in the year.

Make the other team play bad.

And on Monday night at the Caesars Superdome, with his team trailing by 15 at the break, Self again stayed calm, simply emphasizing their defensive mantra and imploring his players to quit playing soft.

As the celebration went on around him after the 72-69 win over North Carolina, Self made his way to the crowd behind KU's bench and asked for his mother, Margaret, to come down. He pulled her in tight.

"Oh, mom," he said. "Wouldn't Dad love this?"

Kansas has one of the greatest pregame hype videos in college basketball, but it hasn't really changed in years. It all leads up to "The Shot" by Mario Chalmers that sent the 2008 national championship game against Memphis to overtime. Jeremy Case, a fifth-year senior on that team, is now a 37-year-old assistant coach on Self's staff, and in recent years, the video has turned a little stale for his tastes.

"2008 was so long ago," he said the day before Kansas beat Villanova in the national semifinals. "We got to quit talking about it. It's like, we still talking about 2008? Damn. They're still showing that video? It's time. We got to get another one."

The urgency was evident this week from Self, who openly talked about the fact that Kansas has banged on that door too many times to have only one national championship to show for his time in Lawrence.

A year ago, you could feel real frustration from Self when his program hit what felt like a low in the NCAA Tournament. USC obliterated Kansas, 85-51, in the second round. It was the most lopsided tournament loss in school history. The Jayhawks had their excuses — mainly, McCormack had just returned from COVID-19 and wasn't himself — but Self didn't hide from what seemed obvious: Talent was the issue.

Recruiting has been hamstrung since the FBI's investigation into college basketball was revealed five years ago, and the NCAA began investigating Kansas a year later. Self had been able to land one of his typical recruiting classes in the Class of 2018 — headlined by top 20 recruits Devon Dotson and Quentin Grimes — but the well dried up after that. Grimes transferred after one season, and Dotson was off to the pros after two. Kansas has not signed a top-20 recruit since then.

On the night of the loss to USC, Self said it had been the downfall of his team all year that the Jayhawks couldn't deal with length and athleticism. He knew the one-time transfer rule was coming, and he saw an opportunity to remake his roster. So when asked that night what he could do to address the issue, he did not mince words, saying recruiting was the answer.

"For us to be a team that really has a chance to be a national contender, we need to get a little bit more athletic," Self said. "We do. And we need to get a little longer and bigger."

The returning players took note of Self's words and the fan response on social media. That night Agbaji gathered the returners and told them to remember the feeling. On Monday night when Agbaji felt panic setting in at halftime, it was Agbaji who spoke up again.

"Guys, just be silent," he said, "and know what you have to do."

They'd been focused on this goal from the time they returned from a short break last April, when strength and conditioning coach Ramsey Nijem wrote the USC score on the whiteboard.

Self and his staff went to work finding speed and shooting those next few months, signing four transfers (Remy Martin, Joseph Yesufu, Jalen Coleman-Lands and Cam Martin) and a freshman point guard (Bobby Pettiford).

And when Kansas made the Final Four, Christian Braun tweeted that afternoon: "That's a lot of trophies for a team that needs to get more athletic."

"We all came back knowing that, 'Man, they don't think this team can get it done. They don't think this team can win championships,'" Braun said this week. "It was just cool for me to see the guys that I played with last year that people didn't think could get it done win all those championships."

What they did, it turns out, was unprecedented.

The Recruiting Services Consensus Index (RSCI) started tracking the cumulative rankings of college basketball recruits in 1999. Since 2001 when that first class tracked were sophomores, every national champion has had at least four top 100 players in its rotation.

Until Monday night.

The Jayhawks won a national title with just two top-100 players in the regular rotation — McCormack (30) and Wilson (51).

You could argue that several Jayhawks would have never even been recruited by Kansas if not for the NCAA case looming over the program for nearly four years now. Agbaji and Wilson were both spring signees, which is usually a time when staffs turn to backup plans. Wilson was originally committed to Michigan and then backed out after John Beilein left to coach the Cleveland Cavaliers. Agbaji at one time considered a post-grad year at Sunrise Christian Academy in Bel Aire, Kansas. Before his senior year of high school, he fell in the mid-major recruit category. Harris was committed to spend a post-grad year at Sunrise in the summer of 2019 when Kansas swooped in and offered the one-time Missouri State commit a scholarship. If not for his friendship with Braun, Harris may have never been a Jayhawk. And if not for the NCAA case, Braun, a sub-100 recruit as well, might have never been a priority.

This week Agbaji said it's important for everyone to run their own race. He wasn't even a starter in his final year of grassroots basketball playing for the Kansas City-based MOKAN program. Braun, who also played for MOKAN, didn't start until the second-to-last tournament of his final year. Harris ended his grassroots career coming off the bench.

"In that basketball world, especially nowadays, there's so much noise when they're growing up with social media and rankings and offers," Drew Molitoris, a MOKAN coach, said. "That derails a lot of kids, because they focus on stuff that's not necessarily important instead of just getting better. And those guys have always just been focused on getting better and winning."

You've got to have pros to win a national title, and this time a year ago it was a reasonable question to ask if Kansas had any. Agbaji and Wilson both tested the NBA Draft waters last spring, but that didn't guarantee they'd one day get drafted. Agbaji ranked in the 90s on Sam Vecenie's draft board for *The Athletic*. Agbaji led KU in scoring as a junior, but no one viewed him as one of the college game's stars.

Agbaji was conscious of his story. He went to Phoenix in the spring to prepare for the draft with Phil Beckner, the NBA trainer famous for training Damian Lillard, and Beckner came away convinced Agbaji was way better than he realized.

"We had to get him to see how good he actually was," Beckner said. "And then see how good he could actually be."

When Agbaji returned home briefly over Memorial Day weekend, he made a trip with his parents to Lawrence to visit Self. Agbaji told Self that day that his mindset had changed. He saw himself as a pro, even if he had to put that off for a year to prove himself to scouts, and he was going to put in the work. It was like he was speaking it into existence,

so he couldn't allow himself to slip below what was now the standard.

In New Orleans, Agbaji played to his pro potential, burying 6-of-7 3s in the Final Four win over Villanova and scoring 12 points in the championship on his way to Most Outstanding Player honors.

While Agbaji was in Phoenix preparing for the draft and getting in the best shape of his life, Braun added 10 pounds. The results were obvious when it took him just 11 games to score more baskets inside the 3-point line than he had in his first two years at Kansas combined. Wilson, who had transformed his body the year before, added a couple inches to his vertical.

Wilson was the talk of preseason practices, excelling in transition and moving with more force than he had before. But three days before KU's exhibition opener, he was cited for driving under the influence. He was suspended for three games and lost his starting spot. When he returned, he wanted to prove his worth and wasn't picking his spots in the right places. In his first 10 games back, he made just 2-of-23 3s and 7-of-18 free throws.

A blessing in disguise for Wilson — and, in reality, the team — was Martin injuring his knee. It allowed Wilson to return to the starting lineup and eventually regain his confidence.

"When he came back, he was not in the best shape because he hadn't played and wasn't in game shape," assistant coach Kurtis Townsend said. "When he was able to start again and started playing like he was capable of playing, that was a big turning point this season."

Wilson says he stopped caring about scoring and simply focused on making winning plays. That's a cliché that gets thrown out around by the players on this team, but it's evident when watching them play.

And it starts with the star. "Ochai doesn't care who scores," Braun said. "Nobody's talking about personal accolades. You see Ochai deflects everything to his team."

This is a theme that's present with most of Self's teams, but it went to an extreme with this group. Molitoris, who has attended a lot of games this year, has a theory. He believes it starts with the parents. Agbaji's father, for instance, told Self on the day he offered his son: "Don't promise this boy any playing time. Whatever time he has to get on the court has to be earned."

"When the parents are about the team, the kids are about the team," Molitoris said. "There is a togetherness that I think is really, really unique, especially in today's age."

Self likes to break the season into segments. There's the pre-Christmas non-conference season when it's sort of a feeling-out period. There's Christmas break, when the rules on practice time go out the window and Self starts to mold his team into what he wants. "That's why we've won so many Big 12 championships," Townsend said. "That's the turning point in the season."

Then there's the conference season and postseason. But Christmastime is as important as any other.

Before Christmas, there was a lot to like. It was evident from opening night at the Champions Classic that this Kansas team was ready to make a leap. Agbaji scored 29 points that night, the opening salvo in a season that ended with him an All-American. Agbaji was hardly recognizable from the player he'd been before. He was so much more confident. He could put the ball on the floor and score from all three levels. He was excelling in transition, an area where his coaches say he was terrible earlier in his career.

Self empowered the Jayhawks in the preseason to run, which was a bold move considering this core had been bad in transition throughout their careers. "It made him crazy," Case said.

But in the preseason, Wilson had been awesome at grabbing rebounds and starting the break himself. Agbaji and Braun also were capable, and then Martin added another dimension of speed so that it just made sense to increase the tempo.

The Jayhawks had a new identity. They were one of the best offensive teams in the country, the numbers and eye test reflecting that. But what frustrated Self was that one of the best defensive teams in the country over the second half of 2020-21 had really slipped on that end. Over Christmas, he challenged Braun and Wilson, in particular, to guard their position and keep the ball in front of them. He also told his team it needed to pay closer attention to the scouting report, and all he had to do was simply point to a late-November loss to Dayton as proof of what could happen when they didn't.

Agbaji, again, was the leader here. Before a mid-February win against Oklahoma State, assistant Norm Roberts was going over a middle ball-screen action that had given the Jayhawks trouble. As the players watched from the baseline, Agbaji spoke up, asking what they were all wondering. "Coach, do you want us to bump the roll man and get back? Or you want me to be the MIG (most important guy) and I stay the MIG, so now when they throw it back, 'Juan is going to take him, and then when they reverse it, I'm going to X-out. How do you want us to guard that?"

"That wouldn't have happened last year," Fred Quartlebaum, KU's direction of basketball operations, said. "That's Ochai Agbaji every day now."

But over the course of a season, slippage occurs, and it happened for Kansas in a March 1 loss at TCU. The Jayhawks were coming off a road loss at Baylor, and to guarantee an outright league title,

they needed to go 3-0 the final week of the season. It wasn't just that they lost to TCU; it was how.

"I don't think we quite took them serious as we should have," Case said. "We underestimated how athletic they were, underestimated how well they rebound the ball, and we just got punked."

Self was fuming after. In the next day in film, he pointed out soft plays — not going after the ball, not following the scouting report. The coaches say he was as hard on the players as he'd been all year.

Agbaji was also frustrated, telling his teammates he wasn't going out like that.

"A lot of teams will shy away from, not necessarily discipline, but Coach getting on their ass," Case said. "They didn't shy away from that. They owned it. And that's the sign of a mature team."

Self likes to talk to this team about his 2019-2020 group that was the favorite to win the national title, in part because it resonates with the players who were on that team. Agbaji, Braun and McCormack were part of the rotation. Mitch Lightfoot, Wilson and Harris were all redshirting.

"Whenever we walked into a gym, we knew there was no doubt," Braun said. "We didn't have to make shots because we were gonna make you play worse than us, no matter what."

That's what became the battle cry after TCU: Make the other team play worse.

Since that loss, the Jayhawks have held their opponents to the 10th-lowest adjusted efficiency in the country, per BartTorvik.com, and it started to feel a lot like 2020.

"After we won the Big 12 regular season — we shared it — and I think everybody looked at each other (like), 'We didn't want to share this,'" Braun said. "Coach said in the interview, we're going to go show everybody who the best team in the Big 12

was. We went and did that in the tournament, and now everybody was looking around, like alright, we could win this. We think we're the best team in the country."

The Jayhawks didn't exactly look the part in the early rounds of the NCAA Tournament when Agbaji was in a slump and he and his teammates were playing tight. Self approached Agbaji after the Sweet 16 win over Providence — when he scored a season-low five points — and told him, "You're due for one."

The Jayhawks played tight in the first half of the next game and were allowing Miami to do everything offensively that they were told not to allow on the scouting report. Self addressed those issues at halftime, making it clear the defense needed to tighten up. For the next 20 minutes, defense led to offense, Agbaji caught fire — scoring 12 second-half points — and it was like all the pent-up nervousness was simply let go.

"We've been as locked in," Self said, "as any team that I can remember."

Kansas has its first five plays of every game pre-planned. The script was off to a beautiful start on Monday night, Kansas jumping out to a 9-3 lead. Of course, it went to hell from there.

But Self delivered a calm message:

"The main thing was that the things that were happening in the first half were correctable," Case said. "We told them to stop being soft. Offensive rebounding, transition defense, the things that we came into the game and said we weren't gonna let them do these things, we could correct those."

Case, the assistant charged with scouting North Carolina, looked at his call sheet at halftime, and the 11 plays he and Self thought would work against the Tar Heels, and they knew the one the Jayhawks needed to start the half.

It's a play called 54, something the Jayhawks put in a few years ago for Dedrick Lawson and Udoka Azubuike (and later Marcus Garrett and Azubuike), an elbow entry and then a pick-and-roll. It'd been so long since the Jayhawks ran it that Case couldn't remember the last time they'd done so, but Self wanted it for this game. The plan was the Jayhawks would get a stop to start the second half — as they did, Agbaji forcing Caleb Love into a travel violation — and Agbaji would bring the ball up, enter it into Harris at the left elbow, McCormack would set the ball screen and then Harris would lob it up to the big man for the dunk.

The Jayhawks were off and running from there, with Self in a play-calling zone as his Jayhawks carved up UNC's defense. When he saw Love hurt his ankle, he went to Braun in the post, a wrinkle of posting up his guards he'd added this preseason.

When Leaky Black went to the bench and Puff Johnson got the Agbaji assignment, Self called a pin down for Agbaji, who drove in for an and-one, tying the game at 50.

Then came Martin. One high-major head coach told Self last offseason that if he took Martin out of the transfer portal, the former Arizona State star could get him to a Final Four. Martin did one better and got his coach a championship. Martin played to his late-season microwave man role, scoring 11 of his 14 points in the second half and banging the 3 from the right corner that gave KU back the lead.

Martin, who at one time was rumored to never be returning from a knee injury, dissected UNC's defense in pick-and-roll again and again down the stretch, scoring when the opportunities presented themselves and finding shooters when the Heels squeezed in.

"What else they want?" Martin screamed as the Jayhawks cut down a second net. "What they say now?"

It wasn't always smooth sailing with Martin this year. It took a while for him to learn what Self wanted out of him and where to be on the floor. In KU's first loss of the season to Dayton, he ran to the wrong spot on a post-up play for McCormack that would have put Kansas up three, giving the Flyers a chance to win it at the buzzer, which they did.

Self ran that same play with Kansas ahead by one in the final minute. Against Dayton, Martin had brought a crowd to McCormack, and he turned it over. This time, with Martin initiating, he ran to the right spot and McCormack had the space to get to his right hook.

"It shows he has unwavering faith in me and belief in me knowing that I will provide when the game was on the line," McCormack said. "Coach tells me all the time we have the inside presence. He knows I can dictate the game, and he proved that and showed that to me going to me with the game on the line."

Self believed McCormack, who scored 15 points two nights after a career-high 25 in the semis, should have shared tournament MOP honors with Agbaji.

That's why he gave him that net. McCormack had given him a championship.

And he beat a UNC program that had been 46-0 in the tournament when leading by double-digits at halftime.

Down nine to Memphis with two minutes left. Down 15 to UNC at half. Self's Jayhawks now have the two greatest comebacks in NCAA Tournament title game history.

"How about that?" Self said as he climbed the stairs for one final team picture. "Boys balled out the second half." ▬▬

'He Worked So Hard for This'

Final Four MOP Ochai Agbaji Earns a Storybook Ending

By Dana O'Neil

APRIL 5, 2022

A brand new national championship hat perched on his head and the confetti still freshly fallen at his feet, Ochai Agbaji sprinted down the steps of the elevated Superdome court and over to the railing where the Kansas fans crowded around for pictures. He looked only upward, motioning with his hand to call to his family to come down to see him. "No, no, come here," he said, a smile spreading on his face. "Come here."

One by one they arrived — first his father, Olofu. "You did it, boy. You did it." Then his mother, Erica. "You're a champion," she said, her voice rising with the final word, equal parts elation and disbelief. "You're a champion." And finally, his sister, Orie, the only one crying. She just wrapped her baby brother in a bear hug, her parents joining in for the family squeeze.

Someone behind Agbaji suggested he make his way back on the court, towards the stage for the trophy presentation. Only then did Agbaji reluctantly separate himself from his family, his own eyes wet with tears. "I love you guys," he said as he returned to the court.

On Feb. 3, 2018, Agbaji turned to his father and incredulously decreed, "Kansas just offered me a scholarship," as if the very idea of such a thing was preposterous. Now four years and two months later, Agbaji paraded under the basket as his teammates took their turns cutting down the net, not just a national champion but the Final Four Most Outstanding Player. Later his coach would rank him as the most accomplished Kansas player since Danny Manning. If anything ranks more improbable than Kansas' resurrection from the dead of a 15-point halftime hole to a 72-69 win over North Carolina and a title, it is Agbaji's role in taking the Jayhawks there.

"Hard work, just hard, hard work," said Olofu, standing at the railing his son had just vacated, bent over at the waist, leaning hard on his hands as if he, too, were exhausted. "That's why I am so proud of him. He worked so hard for this."

The hard work, doubling down with a trainer that nearly sent him to the brink of quitting, and the journey itself, from a burned redshirt season to Naismith candidate, has been well documented and revisited plenty over this Final Four weekend. It still bears remembering now, in the aftermath of this game, because a team doesn't come back the way Kansas came back unless it has a player who understands what it is to keep going when everything else says stop.

Agbaji drained the first bucket of the game, a good-luck 3, and after the Jayhawks jumped to a 7-0 lead, it felt like the game might be heading to Baylor-stomps-Gonzaga territory. North Carolina, after all, was physically depleted, with Armando Bacot playing on one good ankle, and emotionally spent after upsetting Duke two nights earlier. Instead, Kansas went the other way, crumbling into a dysfunctional mess. The wrong guys took all the shots, Agbaji taking his third at the 9:50 mark and not another one until the under four timeout, thanks largely to the defensive blanket Leaky Black tossed on top of him. On the sideline, Bill Self went from angry to exasperated, at one point chuckling derisively as his Jayhawks made like the Keystone Kops and dissolved into the 15-point halftime deficit.

Agbaji knows how that sort of thing goes, how a plan derails. He was supposed to redshirt his freshman season, take the season to get better and stronger. Instead Self burned it in January 2019, as the Jayhawks battled injury and suspension issues. The plan eventually made Self look like a genius, albeit unintentionally, Agbaji steadily growing from an all-league second-team player to first-team All-Big 12 to a player good enough to test the NBA Draft waters last year to a national player of the year candidate.

As March dawned, the presumption rightly was that Agbaji would be that guy, the one who takes over the month and charms the common fan into adoring him. Except Agbaji isn't naturally wired that way. He's nice, deferential even. When a reporter asked him about his local high school, Oak Park, hosting an Och Park Day in his honor he explained that was his nickname in high school. "Other schools would call our school instead of Oak Park, they'd just call us Och Park because everyone knew me," he said. You read that, and it could sound arrogant. You hear Agbaji say it, and it sounds apologetic.

So when the March takeover didn't come, at least not right away, fans fretted and reporters pressed Self about it. The coach never sounded worried, and Agbaji didn't either. Some guys in those situations, they press. They hunt shots and try to force things to happen. He just bided his time, figuring his moment would come when his team needed him most.

This leads us back here, back to this game. A 15-point deficit doesn't turn into the largest comeback in NCAA championship history with a bunch of panickers who try to get it all back in one possession. It takes patience and deliverance and cohesion. It takes a guy such as Agbaji, a star player willing to fit into the offense, not trying to become it, picking his spots, and then exploiting his chances for all that they offer.

His came with just under 11 minutes to go in the game. On the previous possession, with Kansas having chipped away all but the final point of that North Carolina lead and suddenly trailing just 48-47, Agbaji got a great look at an open 3. Sink it, and the place loses its collective mind. Instead the ball rimmed out and Puff Johnson dunked to put the Heels back up three. On the very next possession, with Black out with foul trouble, Agbaji got around the corner, forcing Johnson to have to slide to recover to catch him. He couldn't. Agbaji scored on the drive, drawing the foul as he went up. His free throws brought the Jayhawks all the way back for the 50-50 tie.

Kansas trailed just once more the rest of the game, collecting the school's fourth national title in the hardest way possible in NCAA history. Told about the record deficit that his son and his teammates had just overcome, Olofu Agbaji laughed. "What? Really?" he said. "Well, I'm not surprised. That's who they are. They just work."

A few minutes later, the hard work complete, Agbaji climbed the ladder for his snippet of the net. When he collected the twine, he turned toward the section where his family sat and waved it in their direction. He climbed back down, returning to Earth but his head still in the stars.

Asked what he would have thought if this Monday night scenario were laid in front of him all those years ago, Agbaji, born on the wrong side — the Missouri side — of the Border War first cracked a little joke. "I'd say, 'You're lying,'" Agbaji told The Athletic. "I mean, first all of I'd say, 'Why am I at Kansas, being from Missouri?'"

But then he got serious, glancing over his right shoulder as his teammates danced behind him beneath the ladder. "When I came back last year, my goal was to win everything I could, to win at all costs, and that's what we did. We won the Big 12 regular season. We won the Big 12 tournament. We made it to the Final Four, and now we're national champions. I mean, it's crazy just saying that."

No less crazy a ride than his own. ▬▬

ROAD TO

THE TITLE

At the Start

Kansas is Light on Superstars but is Loaded with Experience and Depth

By CJ Moore
SEPTEMBER 23, 2021

Ochai Agbaji returned to Lawrence this summer after his flirtation with the NBA because he wanted to be a first-round pick. He believes he can make the leap this season, and he's been around long enough to know NBA teams are attracted to winning. So when he got reunited with his old teammates and met his new ones, Agbaji had a message to deliver. Two years earlier, he told them, there was a belief that started in the preseason that the Jayhawks were on a path toward a national title.

"That's what was set in stone from day one," he says. "We actually had that goal. We had a successful season shooting towards something higher than taking it game by game. It was just a mindset thing that carried us a long way that started long before the even the season even began."

Agbaji feels that now, sitting in the captain's chair in September. He believes the 2019-20 team that finished 28-3 and ranked No. 1 in the polls was on its way to winning that national title, and it has been ingrained in the minds of all of his teammates — who all sing the same chorus — that the expectation is to win the Big 12 conference and national titles.

That is player driven, Bill Self will tell you, and he has noticed that the leadership is better than Kansas has had in years. "Because guys are older," he says. "We just seem to be a more confident bunch."

Self is confident in what he's built as well. He says it's different than his past teams because many of those have featured two dominant pieces and role players surrounding them. "This year seems like to me we have more really good players," Self says. "I don't know that we've been this deep with solid players, but I don't think we have the top-heavy lottery pick either."

Self has won with that formula before. It's a little reminiscent of his 2008 national championship team. Those Jayhawks did have a lottery pick (Brandon Rush went No. 13), but the scoring was spread out, and the go-to guy could change game to game.

Self has rarely gone deep into his bench in recent years, but he's talking as though he could play 10 or 11 guys and use that depth to apply more defensive pressure and play faster. This could be all coach-speak, because benches always appear deeper in September. But one reason to believe Self could actually adopt this practice is that he was equipped to move on without Agbaji or Jalen Wilson — who also tested the waters — by landing four upperclassmen transfers. So with Agbaji and Wilson back, this does legitimately look like one of the deepest teams Self has ever coached, with the flexibility to play a lot of different styles.

The big question

The Jayhawks are going to be able to guard. After Self made an adjustment to his ball-screen coverage and made it a priority to keep the ball out of the middle of the floor, Kansas had a nine-game stretch starting in February that was arguably the best defensive stretch for any team in the country last year. And yet ...

"We lost the best defender in the country (in Marcus Garrett), but we're better defensively," Self says. "We should be better defensively."

This is not just preseason optimism. In the years when Self has returned at least four starters at Kansas from the previous season (like this year), his defenses have ranked second, first, first, eighth and third in adjusted defensive efficiency.

The area where the Jayhawks weren't as efficient last year and where they need to improve to be elite is on the other end of the floor. And that's the question mark heading into this season.

The biggest issue for KU's offense was the absence of playmaking guards. That led to a big drop-off in the ability to play out of ball screens, which has become imperative in Self's offense. His offensive formula is pretty simple: put two small playmaking guards on the floor and play around a scoring big in the post.

"We played with one guard last year, for the most part," Self says.

And that one guard was Garrett, who was playing out of position.

In addition to creating post angles, Self's offense has thrived using ball screens to either create for the guards using them or set up a shot for others. Between 2016 and 2020, Kansas ranked in the top 10 percent nationally in ball-screen efficiency in four of five seasons, according to Synergy. All four of those teams scored around one point per possession. Last year, KU's ball-screen efficiency dropped to 0.842 points per trip, which ranked 193rd nationally.

Self believes he addressed this by landing former Arizona State leading scorer Remy Martin, Drake transfer Joseph Yesufu and freshman point guard Bobby Pettiford in addition to returning point guard Dajuan Harris. Harris came on strong the final month of the season, and Self believes he is one of the more improved players in his program. The numbers back up Self's belief that the additions should plug a leak.

Arizona State scored 0.982 points per trip on ball-screen generated offense that involved Martin, and Drake scored 0.965 points per trip in those situations with Yesufu.

"We're gonna be so much better," Self says. "I also think our returning guys will be much better utilizing them."

This has a domino effect for much of KU's offense. When you have guards who can create advantageous situations out of ball screens, the outside shots get better, and there are more easy buckets at the rim. Considering Kansas shot its worst percentage ever from 3 since Self's first season in 2004 and its second-lowest 2-point percentage in his tenure, these are important developments.

Roster analysis

GUARDS: Seven of the last eight national champions have started two point guards, and most of Self's best teams have gone this route. At Illinois, he had Deron Williams and Dee Brown. At Kansas, the national title team paired Mario Chalmers and Russell Robinson (with Sherron Collins as the sixth man). Then it was Collins and Tyshawn Taylor starting together and eventually he had Frank Mason and Devonte' Graham.

Self could do it again this year, and based on how he was aggressively pursuing guards in the spring, the smart money was on Self going that route. But when he was asked last week how often he'd play two little guards at the same time, he said 20 percent. Given more time to think about lineups and rotations, Self would probably up that number a bit. But if you're looking for the logic behind his calculation, it'll lead you to 6-foot-6 junior guard Christian Braun.

Braun was the returning starter most in danger of moving to the bench, but it's hard to see that happening the way Self talks about him now.

"So much, so much stronger, and he seems to be more confident and seems to be better with the ball," Self says. "I'm expecting big things from all these guys, but I'm expecting CB to have a breakout year, so to speak. He had a really good year last year, and he had a really good freshman year. But I think there's a big, big step he can still take and look forward to watching him do it."

Braun, of course, can also play both forward positions, so there is flexibility to get him on the floor along with two smaller guards.

When KU does go small, it'll be some combination of Remy Martin, Joseph Yesufu, Dajuan Harris and Bobby Pettiford. Harris is a better fit on this roster than he was last season, because both Martin and Yesufu are shooting threats. Self figured out ways to make it work with Harris and Garrett, but spacing was always a challenge.

Yesufu has the ball-handling chops to be that second point guard on the floor, but he's really more of a small shooting guard. He's built to score, and he could end up being utilized similar to Collins his first two years at KU when he was instant offense off the bench. That's a similar role that Yesufu played at Drake, where he was the sixth man the first 24 games last season. Yesufu was one of the hottest scorers in the country at the end of last season, averaging 23.2 points over his final nine games. (Seven of those games he started because of an injury to Drake point guard Roman Penn.)

The Jayhawks' depth in the backcourt could make it tough to find playing time for Pettiford and fellow freshman Kyle Cuffe. Self said there are a couple "or more" redshirt possibilities, and Cuffe is likely near the top of that list. Cuffe reclassified from the 2022 class, and it'd make sense for him to sit out this year.

WINGS: Ochai Agbaji is asked which Kansas player has the loudest voice in the room — another way of asking who is this team's leader — and Agbaji confidently answers himself. Everyone around the program has noticed that Agbaji is carrying himself in a different way since returning this summer. He's always worn a smile and been outgoing, but his confidence in his game and his voice is growing.

On the floor, where that could be seen is how Agbaji attacks. Last season he improved his jumper and scored most of his points beyond the arc, knocking down a respectable 37.7 percent from deep. He has gradually improved his handle and his ability to slash throughout his career, but that part of his game isn't something opponents have feared. That's what Agbaji wants to change. Because of the threat of his jumper, he knows his shot fake can be a weapon and help him get to the rim, and once there ...

"I'm just going to try to dunk," he says. "I'm just going to try to go to the rim and jump as high as possible. Just having that mindset continuously is going to turn into a habit."

Both Agbaji and Self believe this approach will help him get to the free-throw line more often, which is something he's never done enough of in his career.

Expected to start alongside Agbaji on the wing is redshirt sophomore Jalen Wilson, who like Braun, has drawn rave reviews from Self for his offseason work.

"He's in unbelievable physical condition," Self says. "He was so much better than he was as a freshman when he came back last year, and he's a lot better than where he was when the season ended. I'm just totally impressed with how hard he's worked, and his skill seems to be better — more consistent shooting the ball — and he is just a more competent, more aggressive basketball player."

Because Self was worried about losing Agbaji or Wilson or both, the Jayhawks found a backup plan in Iowa State transfer Jalen Coleman-Lands, who is at his fourth school. Coleman-Lands started college at Illinois in 2015, and his maturity and professionalism is something that comes up with anyone you talk to around the program. Coleman-Lands has made 293 3s in his career, and his shooting and experience will likely win him a spot in the rotation. His role could be similar to the one played by Isaiah Moss two years ago when he came to KU as a graduate transfer and was used as a sniper off the bench.

Self likes having big wings like Wilson, who allow him to play a more skilled player at the four spot, and he has another option there in freshman K.J. Adams.

"K.J. is a great passer," senior center David McCormack says. "He plays with great energy. Great motor. Plays hard and physical. He's super strong."

BIGS: David McCormack underwent a transformation midway through last season. It went from speculation that Kansas might have been better off by going the extreme small ball route to McCormack becoming the most dominant center in the league.

"I have no problem admitting how slow that first half of the season was for me," McCormack says. "I think that it was just kind of overbearing pressure I put on myself. Once it got to a point it was really just like, 'Yo, screw it. Play your game. Play like you know how to play and just don't think.' And that's really the mindset I'm taking to this year, like you've proven that you can already do it ... just do that all year."

The Jayhawks shouldn't have to be as reliant on McCormack as they became because they have a lot more scoring on the perimeter. Self also has options when McCormack is off. KU added super senior Cam Martin, who was one of the most productive scorers at the Division II level. Martin, who played for former Jayhawks guard Jeff Boschee at Missouri Southern, averaged 25 points and shot 44.5 percent from 3-point range last season.

"Cam is definitely a shooter," McCormack says. "He has great touch and great feel."

Self says he'll use two-big lineups 10 to 15 percent of the time. For reference, that would be way more often than last year. McCormack and Mitch Lightfoot were on the floor at the same time for only 40 possessions, according to Hooplens. com lineup data. Going big this year could be a tricky fit defensively, but offensively both Martin and freshman Zach Clemence are good enough shooters that the Jayhawks should be able to make the spacing work. McCormack says that Clemence has improved more than any player since the summer. He could be another player Self may want to consider redshirting, because there aren't a lot of minutes available in the frontcourt with Self's preference to go small. Plus, in addition to McCormack and Martin, KU also has Lightfoot, the super senior who is entering his sixth year in the program.

Spotlight on: Remy Martin

Asked to describe their new point guard, "speed" is the first word that comes to mind for both McCormack and Agbaji. It's a little reminiscent of playing with Devon Dotson, but their games are not identical. Dotson was like a one-man fast break, McCormack explains. Martin likes to push the pace, but so far McCormack has noticed Martin is looking to pass more and is willing to pull it out if there's nothing there.

That doesn't exactly line up with Martin's reputation at Arizona State, where he was a high-usage scorer. He played fast there too, but his main job was to score.

"I had to do a little bit more at Arizona State — shoot shots that maybe weren't the best shots — but I did it because I felt like that was our best chance," Martin says. "Here I don't think I need to do that. I think people kind of expect me to shoot more here, but I don't need to. For the most part, the game is just penetrate and kick, and we have so many talented guys that anybody could do it on any given night."

The Jayhawks needed Martin for his offensive skill, but Self is also excited by Martin's ability to pressure the ball. Self plans to extend his defense more often and apply more pressure this season, and his hope is that Martin's ball pressure will allow KU's athletes behind him to run through some passes.

It looks like a great pairing on paper. Kansas filled a need, and Martin wanted to play for a winner. He says he never considered another school once he decided to leave Arizona State. It was either stay in the draft or go to KU.

Martin has worked so hard at fitting in so far that Self says he's almost been unselfish to a fault.

"He's got to look to score more than what he has," Self says. "He'll go practices without shooting the ball, just because he wants to just get other guys shots has been his focus."

Martin knows he can flip that switch when he needs to, but he's done what he needs to do so far to win over the room.

And he's definitely winning the press conference with gems like this one that Jayhawks fans will eat up: "People here just want to win," he says. "And I think they're used to winning. Me being a newcomer, I want to carry on that tradition and not let it drop. I want to be able to be a part of this legacy in the right way."

Recruiting

Self has quieted any talk that the NCAA cloud has hindered recruiting. It was a narrative worth pushing the last couple years, but he's already lined up what would be a stellar class by KU's standards no matter the circumstances. The headliners are wings M.J. Rice (ranked No. 22 in the 247Sports Composite) and Gradey Dick (No. 32). They continue Self's pursuit of big, skilled, defensively versatile wings that allow the Jayhawks to go the small-ball route.

Self also landed a four-star big man in Zuby Ejiofor (ranked No. 50 in the class). Projecting any roster going forward with the new one-time transfer rule, in addition to the COVID-19 exception that gave all players who played last season an extra year of eligibility, is difficult. For instance, both Agbaji and McCormack could conceivably play two more seasons. But most likely, both Agbaji and McCormack will be playing their final season. Lightfoot, both Martins and Coleman-Lands will run out of eligibility. Lightfoot doesn't count against the scholarship limit this year, so if Kansas loses just those six players, it would have just two more scholarships left. Self and his staff are still aggressively recruiting 2022 high schoolers and will likely be able to plug holes on the transfer market again in the spring.

Schedule analysis

This is a typical Kansas schedule with several high-profile nonconference matchups and then a Big 12 slate that will boost all the important numbers that the selection committee cares about. The Jayhawks open at the Champions Classic in New York against Michigan State. Over Thanksgiving weekend, they travel to Orlando for the ESPN Events Invitational, where they'll open against North Texas, which upset Purdue in the NCAA Tournament last season. The second game will be against either Dayton or Miami, and KU could potentially meet Alabama or Drake in the championship game. Both should be NCAA Tournament teams this year.

Kansas has a pair of road games in December at St. John's (Dec. 3) and Colorado (Dec. 21), and the highlight of December will be the return of the Border War on Dec. 11 at Allen Fieldhouse.

The Jayhawks will also play Kentucky again this year in the Big 12/SEC Challenge. The Wildcats, who will likely be ranked in the Top 10 in the preseason, travel to Lawrence on Jan. 29. One other thing that pops on the schedule is Senior Day is against Texas on March 5. Chris Beard has a stacked roster, and it'll be the second straight season where the Senior Day winning streak (now at 38) could be in real jeopardy. (Last season the Jayhawks played then-unbeaten Baylor on Senior Day and pulled off the upset.)

The ceiling

This roster appears to have everything. Remy Martin and Yesufu were the missing pieces on the perimeter, and you can never have enough shooting. Self got more of it in Cam Martin, Coleman-Lands, Martin, Yesufu and Clemence.

It'll be tough to keep everyone happy with playing time, but Self is pretty good at managing a roster and not letting feelings get in the way of pursuing championships. A national title is what the players say they're after, and if McCormack is second-half-of-last-season McCormack, if Martin can fit in and be a more efficient version of the dude who played at Arizona State, and if the Agbaji-Braun-Wilson trio make the gradual improvements that have come to be expected in KU's program, then, yes, that sounds good enough to win a national title.

As Kansas fans know, the best team doesn't always win in the NCAA Tournament. But the luxury Self should have is the ability to match up against any team stylistically. And if Self really does use his bench like he says he plans to, then the Jayhawks may just be able to wear opponents down.

The floor

Self said it himself: he has a lot of really good players, but he doesn't have the one or two dominant forces he's used to rostering. That was basically the case last season, and on some nights offensively the Jayhawks looked like a team without an identity. Early on they needed the 3 to fall to look good, and then late they had to have McCormack rolling. In the end, they were simply overwhelmed by a team, USC, that did have a lottery pick, Evan Mobley.

The offense should be better, but the lack of a true star could mean some off nights. The hope for Self should be that these additions lead to an offense that finds itself in the top 10 in efficiency. It's hard to win a national title if you're not elite on both ends, and maybe this is an offense that's better but finds itself in the high 20s or low 30s.

The Jayhawks are going to win a lot of games, but it's no longer a given that they win the league every year. Baylor, Texas and even Texas Tech appear to be formidable threats. The floor for this group is probably third or fourth in the Big 12, around a No. 3 or 4 seed in the tourney and another tourney exit to a team with a lottery pick on it.

Final report

Self's best teams usually have a core that has been together for a couple years. That's college basketball. Teams need to marinate. Look at Baylor last year. It wasn't just that the Bears had high-end talent. It's that they grew together. They wouldn't have been as great if they'd been thrown together the summer before.

Of course, we've also seen a team in the Big 12 add some important transfer pieces to a good core

group and make the national title game. That was Texas Tech in 2019. KU is returning four starters, so it's not like this is a completely new group. Self smartly plugged the holes by adding Remy Martin and Yesufu, and he has a returning group that is really hungry after missing out on the 2020 tourney and then getting smoked by USC in 2021.

That core also has experienced playing on a national championship-caliber team. Self is hesitant to say he gets 2019-2020 vibes with this crew, but the players sense it.

"I can feel that within this team and feel how connected we are on and off the court, which is definitely going to help us go a long ways," McCormack says. "I have that same confident feeling in us, that same sense of team determination and discipline."

And if you're looking for one last team comp to feel good about this crew: North Carolina won a national title in 2017 in the midst of a stretch when

it was believed Roy Williams wasn't recruiting at his typical level because the Tar Heels were dealing with their own NCAA mess. That was a collection of really good players without a surefire lottery pick, but they were old and hungry after losing in the title game the year before.

It's not apples to apples, but there's a lot of similar themes with these 2021-22 Jayhawks. ▰▰

Bill Self

'The Little Things' Drove the Jayhawks' Comeback Win Against Kansas State

By CJ Moore

JANUARY 22, 2022

Bill Self Sr. would never blow up at his kids about the big stuff. Only the small stuff. "If you're late for curfew or if you let your car run out of gas, oh yeah, he'd go off on you," Bill Self Jr. said. "But anything that was big? Calm. Never rattled."

The younger Self, the coach for the University of Kansas, coached the first game of his life without his dad on Saturday against Kansas State. The elder Self, 82, died Friday at his home in Edmond, Okla., surrounded by his family.

Self has been telling that story for years to his players and assistant coaches. "That always stuck with me," Barry Hinson, Self's first assistant at Oral Roberts, said when reached on Friday afternoon. "It is the one thing that Bill Self Sr. did that has helped me as a parent."

Hinson watched his friend build programs with that approach. Self lost 15 consecutive games to

finish his first season at Oral Roberts in 1994, but he just kept chipping away at the finer points. He obsessed over the little things. The details. By his third year, he had a winner. From there, he built a Hall of Fame career by simply coaching those details as well as anyone in America and never getting stuck on the big stuff.

"People, they always ask you, 'What is it about Bill Self?'" Hinson said. "When you watch him coach during the game, a guy turns it over, misses a free throw, block out, doesn't go to the glass, doesn't guard, doesn't dive on the floor, doesn't take a charge, he goes nuts. But a guy takes a bad shot or misses a shot at the end of the game to win it ... I think you'd go back to the teaching that his dad gave him. I really believe it. I think it all goes back to his dad."

Hinson, of course, had no idea what was going to go down inside Bramlage Coliseum against rival Kansas State. Self's team trailed by 16 at halftime,

as the Wildcats played the best half of their season and star Nijel Pack caught fire. It would have been easy to flip over a table at halftime and really let his team have it.

Self kept his cool. He told himself going into the game that he was never going to get mad, and he reminded himself as the lead grew. "Just keep grinding," he told the Jayhawks.

At halftime, Self told his team it was a learning experience and to look at the big picture. "We got to do the little things right," assistant coach Norm Roberts said when asked what the message was. "We've got to go after the ball with two hands."

Self said he also told his team: "Guys, this will be the most fun locker room all year if we just go out and execute."

The Jayhawks never panicked. Instead, they began nailing those little things. David McCormack

and Jalen Wilson fought for every rebound like it was the last possession. KU had more offensive rebounds (18) than K-State had defensive rebounds (16). KU's ball-screen defense had been dreadful in the first half, so Self tinkered. K-State point guard Markquis Nowell got wherever he wanted to go in the first half; in the second half, it was harder for him to get downhill.

Dajuan Harris stuck like glue to Pack, who still scored 13 second-half points after scoring 22 in the first half, but Pack had to really work for them after halftime. Self played it through his head afterward and could think of only one breakdown.

"I think he saw throughout the whole entire game, even when we're down, our emotions, our attitudes throughout. We were staying poised, focusing on what was at task," senior star Ochai Agbaji said. "Next play. Next possession."

The lead kept shrinking, and the Jayhawks seemed to get better as the pressure increased. Agbaji sank two free throws with 55 seconds left to cut the lead to one. After a stop, Kansas got the ball back with a chance to win. Agbaji had keyed a comeback in the previous game against Oklahoma by burying two 3s late on smart play calls by his coach, the second of which was the result of Self knowing how the Sooners wanted to guard an action and using their plan against them. When Self tried to dial up a play for Agbaji at the end of this game, Agbaji simply had to make a play himself. K-State stopped the initial action, but the ball still found Agbaji, and he spun around and drove to the basket, avoiding help defender Selton Miguel. Had he charged, it would have been a K-State win. Avoiding a charge is something Self has preached since the loss to Texas Tech earlier in the month. The Jayhawks, not surprisingly, did not commit a single charge Saturday.

The details mattered.

When his career is finished, history will look back on this game as one of Self's masterpieces. It will certainly stick out in his mind forever. Minutes after the 78-75 win, once he finished addressing the team, Self came racing out of the visiting locker room and let out a big "whew" as his assistants followed behind him.

"I think he was as excited as any game I've been around," Roberts, who has coached by Self's side for 21 years, said afterward. "The way we won the game and how we had to fight to come back and how the team grew as a team, I think it's really important to him."

Self's father, of course, was on his mind. His dad, who battled rheumatoid lung disease, got pneumonia over Christmas and then caught COVID-19 at the hospital. It became apparent last weekend that his father would not survive, and Self traveled to Edmund on Sunday to be with him. He returned to the Jayhawks on Tuesday to coach at Oklahoma, and Self's father wasn't happy with him for missing practice. "You won't have your team ready," he told his son.

The Jayhawks won on Tuesday, but it wasn't one of their crispest performances. Self then returned to his father, and it looked like he'd made a positive turn late in the week, so Self headed home. But as soon as he got there, he got word that his dad had taken another turn. He headed back to Oklahoma and was there for his dad's final moments Friday morning.

Self didn't want his players to play for him or his dad, but he could tell this game meant more to them. Tuesday, they had moments when it looked like each guy took a turn trying to play hero until finally executing down the stretch. This comeback was won possession by possession with a team approach.

"He was saying at the end of the game there that we had a lot of poise," Agbaji said.

Self Sr. spent his career in education and athletics, first as a teacher and a coach. We all go through life wanting to make our parents proud, and Self has always coached in a way his father would appreciate.

His dad was a grinder, he said. He told his son to always make the most of every situation, even when it doesn't look good.

"He would have respected how hard the kids tried," Self said. "That would have been special for him. Everybody goes through things, but you find out things later on sometimes about how much things that you do impact your own family, and especially him. You know, he hung on to every pass and every basket."

Self's lips started to quiver, each word harder and harder to get out. "And so it was important," he said, finishing his thought before the tears came.

Hinson, now on staff at Oklahoma State, was at practice Friday when Self called to tell him the news. He was happy his friend could return to his team without having to worry about whether he was doing the right thing by coaching. "Because his dad would have whooped his ass if he wouldn't go coach that game," Hinson said.

When Hinson finally talked to Self, he planned to tell him his dad lived a great life.

"He impacted people's lives," Hinson said. "He changed people's lives for the better. And he raised a hell of a son and a hell of a daughter."

And on this particular day, his lessons lived on through his son, and it helped him win yet another game. ▬▬▬

Banner Day

How a Kansas Student Honored Bill Self's Late Father and Gave a Nod to the Jayhawks' Past

By CJ Moore

JANUARY 25, 2022

Kansas junior Aaron Martin's girlfriend thought he was a little crazy on Monday afternoon when he turned her garage into his own art studio and went to work on a giant banner honoring Bill Self's father for the Texas Tech game.

The sign would read, "Just load the wagon," the second part of a quote that means so much to Self that he had the words — "Don't worry about the mules, just load the wagon" — inscribed on his Hall of Fame bench in Springfield, Mass.

This weekend @KUHoops posted the quote and a video documenting the memorable Kansas State win on Saturday. Martin brings a homemade white board to every game to hold up messages — like "Prison Mitch" or "It's Teahan Time" — and he planned to bring a new sign with Bill Sr.'s now famous words. His camping group (You're Dajuan I want) had won the lottery and would be at the front of the line to enter Allen Fieldhouse, meaning Martin would have prime seats to show his creation.

Then on Monday, he was convinced to go bigger than originally planned. KU grad Mike Vernon, a former Bleacher Report employee who tweets frequently about his Jayhawks, tweeted a picture of the bench and wrote, "Do it big today, students."

Martin replied to the tweet, "Working on it, Mike."

Martin, aware of the history of the "Beware of the Phog" banner that hangs in the north rafters, came up with a plan to pay tribute to Self and the former students who made that banner in 1988. Those architecture students devised an elaborate plan to steal shower curtains from McCollum Hall for their canvas. McCollum was bulldozed a few years ago, so Martin opted for Walmart. After finishing his homework around 1 p.m. Monday, he rushed to the store for materials. He found a shower curtain, but he theorized the nylon material on this particular model would make the paint run and smear. Instead, he opted for two twin-sized bed sheets.

He raced back to his girlfriend's and began the process. He mocked up a rough draft on two loose leaf papers and decided he didn't have enough space for the entire quote.

The second half of the quote would work perfectly — 16 letters on a 16-foot-wide canvas. After he finished painting, he went to check on what the finished product looked like and around 4:30 p.m. — 3 1/2 hours before tipoff — he began to panic. The paint hadn't dried yet.

So he decided to open the garage, hoping the outside air would help. He ran home to his house five minutes away to grab more supplies, and while he was gone, the wind had picked up the sheets and folded them over. The blue outline leaked onto the white background and into the red interior, creating splotches of purple. His girlfriend, Natalie Heinbach, had discovered the issue right before he returned and was beginning to repair it. Martin was worried. He didn't have time to start over.

It's around this time she began to question what in the heck was his motivation for going to such great lengths. That's when he showed her a short ESPN documentary about the original banner with home video footage of those architecture students creating their masterpiece in 1988.

"Oh," Heinbach said. "This is so cool."

The original banner-makers hung their creation for the Duke game on Feb. 20. KU lost in overtime, so the students worried it was a jinx and took it down. For Danny Manning's Senior Day that year, they decided to hang it back up. The Jayhawks won and went on to avenge the Duke loss in the Final Four and claim the national title.

After that season, the group graduated and tried to give the banner to Phog Allen's granddaughter. She didn't have space for the 30-foot-wide banner, so she asked the athletic department if they'd want to hang it permanently. Eventually a newer replica took its place, but the banner has had a home in the north rafters since the 1988-89 season.

Those students had an athletic department connection to get their banner in. Martin had no such connection. So around 5 p.m. Monday, he cold-called the athletic department. Whoever answered his call was interested and went to work checking to see if it could happen. Meanwhile, Vernon got in touch with former KU media relations employee Adam Sullivan, who showed a donor, who showed deputy AD Sean Lester, who had associate athletic director Drew Gaschler reach back out to Martin.

When Martin sent Gaschler pictures of his creation, Gaschler was sold. "It just looked kind of natural — fan-made, really authentic," Gaschler said. "We encourage fans to be creative and for them to feel like they're part of the program."

A plan was put in place. They would hang the banner in front of the student section on the south side. Martin just had to get it there — a 1/2 mile walk from Heinbach's garage off Louisiana Street to the Allen Fieldhouse entrance.

"It was kind of stressful, because I had to fold it up," Martin said. "It's about a 10-minute walk. It felt dry, but I was worried that once I got there and unfolded it that it was just gonna be like all smushed. But we got there, unfolded it and it looked the same."

His creation, made in about four hours, had a prominent spot in the most storied building in college basketball.

The night was made even more special, because Martin's brother, Nathan, is a graduate assistant for Texas Tech, and their family sat behind the Red Raiders bench on Monday night.

Martin, who fell in love with the Jayhawks when he was 9 during the national championship season, sat right behind the U in his banner. I snapped a picture of it and tweeted it out just over an hour before tip, and soon Martin was tagged and his notifications went crazy.

"My phone was just blowing up," he said. "People were talking about hanging it in the rafters. I'm like, what?! That's crazy. This is not going on. What the heck?"

Martin wanted to make sure Self saw it. Self wasn't able to see it during the game, but he was shown a picture following his press conference.

"Everybody's been so nice to us," Self said. "I know everybody goes through similar things, and so many people have been through so much more than what I have or what my family has, but everybody's been so nice. And we are very appreciative to all the well wishes and the thoughts and prayers. And I know my mom is overwhelmed by it."

After the game, Martin started folding it up when Gaschler approached him and said KU might want to keep the sign around. It's currently sitting in Gaschler's office, and it may return for a future game.

Because Martin made it in about four hours, he knows it could be better. He is not sure whether he'd like to clean it up or make a better version, or stick with the original.

"It is kind of cool that there are mess-ups on it and it's not perfect," he said.

Whether it will get a permanent home inside Allen Fieldhouse is still undecided, but the parallels are kind of eerie to original student-made banner. Each made its debut during overtime games — Kansas won in a double-overtime thriller on Monday — and the first was during Danny Manning's National Player of the Year senior season. And on Monday, senior Ochai Agbaji had a performance that may have vaulted him to the front of the NPOY race.

No matter the banner's final home, Martin has a memory he'll never forget on a night that will go down in Fieldhouse lore. ▰▰

Christian Braun

Rock, talk, Jayhawk: Backing Up Swagger with Star-Level Production

By CJ Moore

FEBRUARY 3, 2022

There are two Christian Brauns. Off the court, he's "more reserved and quiet," his dad says.

"So respectful," Kansas coach Bill Self says.

And then there's the Christian Braun on the court ...

"Bro," Jayhawks teammate Ochai Agbaji says, "he's a whole different guy. He's like an asshole."

The examples are starting to pile up. We got a sneak peek in last year's Champion's Classic, when Braun dunked on former Kentucky big man Isaiah Jackson's head and called him a not-so-nice word on the way down. Earlier this season, a similar scene played out against Dayton, when Toumani Camara was the on-your-head victim. Braun paused when he landed and pointed at Camara to make sure everyone knew he was the one. There was the game at Kansas State two weeks ago, when after about three hours of listening to "F— KU" chants, Braun raced to get the basketball as the buzzer sounded and tossed it into the crowd. And then, of course, there were the courtside hecklers at Oklahoma whom Braun had words for after he buried the game-deciding 3.

That scene in Norman resembled something that took place 30 years ago when his mom, Lisa, was a guard at Missouri, and the OU student section, known as the Roughnecks, used to call her Miss Maybelline. "They'd talk shit to us all game," says Lisa Braun (nee Sandbothe). "When you hear it over and over and over, and you hit a shot like that, it's just the natural reaction."

Christian gets his orneriness from mom. His on-court feistiness is a lot like that of Lisa and her brother, Mike, an enforcer at Missouri in the late 1980s. "Very competitive," Lisa says. "Sometimes our competitiveness comes out of our mouth."

This season, it has come pouring out of Braun. The junior wing has earned the right to be a little pompous. He's gone from spot-up shooter/dirty work guy to a rim-hating slasher/dirty work guy. That second part of the equation will never

change. That's the Sandbothe in him. Self raves about his toughness and calls him the best player he's ever been around at tracking down 50-50 balls, an attribute that is like Bill Self catnip.

Self also loves guys who show some personality on the floor. He'd rather reel them in than have to pump them up. In fact, the coach is Braun's No. 1 needler. They go back and forth constantly in practice. Self will ask him if he's going to make a shot today. "Damn," Self will say. "Waiting on you."

After Braun proceeds to make four in a row, he'll fire off a smart-ass comeback. "I think that's four in row if I'm not mistaken."

"He's that guy all the time," Self says.

The rest of the country is seeing it now. Braun is approaching college basketball villain status. Self even brings up former Mizzou guard Jason Sutherland, who was probably the most hated man in the history of the old Big Eight. When the possibility of Braun becoming KU's version of that guy comes up, he grins out of the side of his mouth. "I like that feeling," he says.

"Loooooooves it," Self says.

"It fuels him," Lisa says.

If Christian Braun is going to be the guy that his fan base loves and everyone else, especially rivals, hate, then let's give the people what they want. Let's talk about Missouri.

Braun comes by his disdain for the Tigers naturally. He was born in what they like to call a "split" household in these parts. They used to make license plates and flags that had a Jayhawk and a Tiger for such families. Lisa was a Tiger. Donny Braun, Christian's father, graduated from Kansas, where he walked on to the basketball team after transferring from Saint Louis. His one regret is he quit during the 1992-93 season to focus on his studies — he'd go on to become a doctor — and that was the year KU made a Final Four. "One of the more stellar moves of my life," he says. Nonetheless, he loved KU basketball.

The Braun kids were split. The oldest boy, Parker, latched onto Mizzou. Christian loved the Jayhawks. It didn't hurt that he was growing up in Burlington, Kansas, and local star Tyrel Reed played at KU. Reed's sister, Lacie, babysat the Brauns, and Tyrel used to come over to play basketball with the boys. He even brought Cole Aldrich to Christian's seventh birthday.

At Christmas time, the Brauns put up a small tree that had both Kansas and Missouri decorations. Eventually, it had to be a KU-only tree, because Christian, according to Lisa, would take off the Missouri ornaments and stomp them.

Parker spent his first three years playing for the Tigers, but he was never able to get consistent minutes and transferred this offseason to Santa Clara, where he's starting for a team that owns wins over TCU, Stanford and BYU.

Christian was frustrated that Parker never really got a chance at Mizzou. He thought his brother would show flashes when he'd get on the floor, and he'd call Parker and ask, "Why aren't you playing?"

From the stories his brother told him, Christian was convinced the Mizzou coaches didn't think Parker was tough enough. He grew up playing in a small rural town and then the suburbs of Kansas City.

"I felt like it maybe it was a grit thing," Christian says. "Maybe it was a toughness thing. Maybe it was something that they thought guys didn't have that where he grew up. I took it personally."
Christian doesn't want this to sound disrespectful — he says he has a lot of respect for Tigers coach Cuonzo Martin — but he wanted to prove a point when the two teams met in Lawrence on Dec. 11.

His plan was to wait until Kansas had a 10-point lead before he said a word. But about a minute into the game, he found himself open in front of the Mizzou bench and fired in a 3. He couldn't help himself. His head swiveled right toward that bench, and the talking started. "I just can't keep it in," he says. "I don't know what it is."

Next possession: an Agbaji 3. More Braun barking. Another minute later, Braun blocked a shot and then made an and-one layup in transition, ending up sliding on his butt along the baseline, turning toward the student section and banging his chest. The camera cut to his parents. Donny, the quieter one, was making his statement by wearing a Santa Clara shirt. Lisa was talking right along with her son.

Braun scored eight of KU's first 11 points, had three assists and forced a shot-clock violation all before the second media timeout. He let out so much emotion in that opening stretch that he was exhausted. Obviously, all the buckets felt good, but it was the way he played in Kansas' 102-65 victory— the hustle plays, keeping his chest in front of ball handlers, grabbing loose balls — that really made his point.

"I thought it was my job to show them (what they were missing)," Braun says. "I really wanted to show them that it doesn't really matter where you're from. If you love basketball, if you play hard, you can have grit. And I think I showed them that."

———————— ————————

Christian Braun has always wanted the last word. An old youth coach calls him "The Attorney," because he refuses to lose an argument. Parker used to sit next to his brother on car rides and wonder why he wouldn't just shut up. "Anything (Lisa) had to say, he had an answer for," Parker says. "She would reach back and just want to slap him in the back of his head. Christian wants to get the last word, but she does too. So once they get going, it's tough to stop."

Once in the fifth grade, when Lisa was coaching the boys, he made the mistake of running his mouth to his mom after messing up in a game. She told him to sit his butt on the bench. He kept going. She told him to go to the end of the bench. He kept going. She handed someone her car keys and told him, "Get your ass to the truck now. Don't come back in."

"Nothing's changed," Donny says, laughing as they recall the story. "She just sends him to his own car now."

They're both stubborn, but Lisa's hard coaching shaped him. Christian feared no one, and he did everything on the floor that coaches loved — taking charges, diving for loose balls, you name it. There was no fake hustle, because his mom would see right through that.

"Coach Self can't shock me with anything he's going to say," Christian says, "because my mom has said worse."

It made him prepared for any battle, internal or external. On the floor, he spent most of his childhood as the little guy. When he started playing for the Kansas City grassroots outfit MOKAN, current teammate Dajuan Harris towered over him. (Harris, for those unaware, is one of the smallest guys in the Big 12.)

As a freshman in high school, Christian was only 5-foot-8. It ended up paying off because he developed as a point guard, and that likely would have gone differently if he'd always been the tall kid. In Burlington, his size didn't matter because he was still one of the best players, but the Brauns went seeking the best competition for their boys. That's why Christian joined MOKAN in seventh grade, and why the Brauns moved to Overland Park at the start of Christian's freshman year.

With MOKAN, the coaches considered demoting him from the top team, but they ended up deciding he could handle not playing as much.

"There were times where I was not good, but I still wanted to compete," Braun says. "I went through times where I'd sit the bench, didn't get in, but every time I got on the court, I thought I was the toughest dude out there."

Braun proved that was the case in the summer between eighth and ninth grade when he broke his hand going for a loose ball. The fracture required the insertion of a screw. Once he had the procedure done, he would have to sit out for a while. He refused, playing the rest of the summer season with the broken hand and putting off surgery.

His right wrist bothered him over the last couple months of last season. His parents would tell him to go have it examined. "He doesn't want to know," Lisa says. "He's like, if I can get through it, I'll be all right."

Braun has not missed a game in college, and Self says he never misses practice.

"I don't know that the dude has taken two possessions off since he's been here in practice," Self says. "He gets hit in the mouth, he gets a knee to the thigh, he gets the wind knocked out of him, and he won't even think about going to see a trainer."

Braun's emotional toughness was tested when Lisa decided to move the boys to Overland Park. It's something the Brauns had considered for a while, and Lisa made the executive decision while Donny was on a business trip, renting an apartment near Blue Valley Northwest, considered one of the best basketball programs in the city, and enrolling the boys. Their first day was the second day of school.

They didn't know anyone and would meet up between classes to say hello to each other, then spend the rest of the day not talking to anybody.

Christian never questioned it. If it was best for his basketball development, then he was all for

it. In Burlington, he would have been the big fish in a small pond. At BVNW, he split time between the freshman and junior varsity teams. As a sophomore, he was the ninth man and didn't play a lot on a state championship team. He never questioned the process, always willing to wait his turn.

His turn came in his junior year. Eight games into that season, with BVNW at 4-4, coach Ed Fritz moved him to point guard, and the Huskies won 17 straight and repeated as state champions.

It was that summer that Braun finally elevated himself to starter for MOKAN and a player that Kansas would actually recruit. It wasn't just because he was the hometown kid. He'd sprouted to 6-7, and 6-7 guys with ball skills will play at the high-major level. But it was the intangibles and his swagger that sold Self. "I always thought he thought he was the best player on every court," Self says.

The true Braun really came out his senior season at BVNW, where he was the unquestioned star and leader. During timeouts, Fritz would talk for about 45 seconds and then leave the final 20 seconds for Braun.

"CB would hold you accountable," Fritz says. "He's not afraid to call out a teammate. He's not afraid to call out himself. He's not afraid to call out a coach, and it's all for the betterment of the team."

Fritz says he's only coached three or four players with a presence like Braun; one of them was Clayton Custer, who went on to play point guard at Loyola Chicago and lead the Ramblers to the Final Four.

While Braun delivered the truth, he also expected it in return. During his recruitment, he hated the approach of most coaches, who would promise shots, playing time and anything else they thought he'd want to hear.

"That's what I loved about Coach Self, because he was completely honest," he says. "I wanted to come here my whole life, so whatever he told me was going to be great. He told me, 'Hey, Christian, I'm going to be honest with you. I'm not gonna promise you a minute, a shot. I'm not going to promise you a single thing.'"

Braun was a four-star recruit, but his signing wasn't one that got KU fans going crazy. The way he remembers it, most fans thought he'd end up redshirting. Instead, he played 18.4 minutes per game as a freshman and even started five games. That was quite the accomplishment, considering the Jayhawks ended that COVID-19 shortened season ranked No. 1 and were the favorite to win the national title.

Braun was so good shooting the ball as a freshman — he made 45.6 percent of his 3s — that his reputation became that of a spot-up shooter who made the hustle plays. He filled the same responsibility as a sophomore, though his shooting numbers dropped a bit. He wasn't displeased with his role — "I adjusted to what we needed," he says — but he felt like he was capable of more.

"His goal was not to be a hometown hero," Lisa says. "His goal is to go to the next level."

To take the next step, he needed to get back to playing more like he did in high school. But listen to how he explains it. Some players come off suggesting that someone else held them back.

Braun?

"It wasn't something that the coaches made me into," he says. "I felt like, I need to go be athletic and go be who I was. It's not even just going and making plays off the bounce; it's just making dunks and highlight plays like that, showing off athleticism."

Self told him to make sure he spent his offseason working on the things that would allow him to show it off in games, so that was his focus.

It's obvious to anyone who has watched Kansas play this year that Braun has succeeded. It took only 11 games for him to make more 2s than he'd made his first two seasons combined. He's thrived in transition and as a cutter. Among players who have finished at least 20 possessions off a cut, he's the eighth-most efficient on those plays (scoring 1.654 points per possession) in the country, per Synergy. That's usually the territory of big men who finish a lot of lobs and dump-offs. The counting stats — 15.1 points, 5.7 rebounds, 3.2 assists and more than a block and a steal per game — are strong as well. Braun has scored in double digits in 19 of 21 games this season for Kansas.

All that has resulted in Braun showing up on mock drafts.

Self says Braun is playing exactly how he wants him to play with one exception. "I wish he'd look for his shot a little bit more," Self says.

Reed, once a hero to Braun, now sees him regularly. The former Jayhawks guard is a physical therapist and works with the team, which allows him to attend many practices and sit back and observe. One thing he's noticed with Braun is that every teammate looks at him like he's their best friend.

"Everyone wants to play with him," Reed says. "Everyone wants to hang around him."

We're all drawn to confidence, and Braun obviously has that. But while he comes off as somewhat cocky on the floor, it's more understated around his team. Self says Braun is always talking up other guys.
 "A sign of true confidence is not being jealous of anybody," Self says. "He's that guy."

It's the perfect dynamic with this year's Jayhawks. Agbaji is the best wing in college basketball, but he's never one to promote himself. It's OK, because he's got Braun to do that for him. Every opportunity Braun gets, he praises Agbaji. In an interview for this story, Braun ended up gushing about how good Agbaji has been and why.

Agbaji is by default this team's leader because of his age, wisdom and talent, but the Jayhawks take their emotional cues from Braun. Even Agbaji has shown more emotion in recent weeks, letting out some screams after big buckets.

With Braun, the noises are a little different. "He'll be talking crazy," Agbaji says, so much so that Braun cannot even recall what he said after the fact.

"I just enjoy the moment," he says. "I don't shy away from it."

He also doesn't shy away from taking on all the venom from an opposing fan bases. And Harris has a warning for those who take the bait.

"They're going to have to deal with it," Harris says, "because that's a bad boy." ▬▬

Ochai Agbaji

Tearful Conversations, 'Hauling Ass' and Damian Lillard:
On Becoming an All-American

By CJ Moore

FEBRUARY 24, 2022

Ochai Agbaji was about to walk out of the gym. He'd never done that before, it occurred to him. Never turned his back on a coach. Never even considered disobeying authority. But Phil Beckner, the NBA trainer tasked with preparing Agbaji for the 2021 draft process, had struck a nerve.

One of Beckner's rules is to always show up to his gym 10 minutes early, ready to go. That means shoes on, stretched. When it's morning time, you better have had breakfast. On this particular Saturday morning, though, Agbaji had walked in eight minutes before start time, wearing slides. He'd skipped breakfast. Forget being properly hydrated. He was barely awake.

"It looked like he'd just rolled out of bed," Beckner's assistant, Hasten Beamer, says.

Beckner told Agbaji to go to the other side of the gym while he started the workout. Agbaji, whom Kansas coach Bill Self calls the sweetest kid in America, had always felt like a hard worker. He always thought he was about the right things. Beckner was the first one to really question that. He wasn't living up to the standard that Beckner expects. That morning, Agbaji had heard enough.

As Beckner approached, Agbaji told himself he wasn't going to take any of it this day. He stood his ground, looked Beckner in the eyes, said, "Just train me."

"What do you think I'm doing?" Beckner asked him.

"You're coaching me," Agbaji said, tears welling up in his eyes. "You're not my coach. Just train me."

Then came three words Agbaji never thought he'd hear himself say.

"I hate you."

Agbaji started to walk out, but thought better of it. He let Beckner have his say. They went back and forth. Beckner asked why he was there. Agbaji told him: Because this was the training he wanted, but Beckner was being too hard on him. Beckner explained why he'd been so hard. He believed Agbaji could be an NBA first-round pick — either that summer or next. "He wouldn't believe me," Beckner says.

Beamer worked the other players out on the other end of the floor while Beckner and Agbaji kept talking. The Kansas star poured it all out. They talked for an hour and a half straight.

Nine months later, Agbaji is on his way to becoming an All-American. Mock drafts project him to be a late lottery pick. He's made plays this season he never dreamed of making before. He knows he's earned the right to be a star.

"He made the choices he needed to make instead of the choice he wanted to make," Beckner says. "And that's why he made the jump. He made some really hard choices of how hard he's gonna work, what he's gonna do, how much he gets confronted, and he deserves this, man."

On their first Sunday together in Phoenix, Beckner took Agbaji to his church, then out for brunch at The Cheesecake Factory. It was a get-to-know-you meal. Agbaji shared his desire to get better and told his basketball story. He'd never been the chosen one. He was once so lightly recruited that his dad wrote letters to coaches at Missouri, Texas and Wichita State to try to get those coaches to at least give him a look. Three straight years he tried out and failed to make MOKAN, the Nike-sponsored grassroots team in Kansas City. He finally made it the summer before his senior year, but he wasn't a star. He was considered a mid-major recruit, and before his senior season, even Missouri State and Northern Iowa were wavering in their interest.

On the day that Self offered him a scholarship — Feb. 3, 2018, following a loss to Oklahoma State at Allen Fieldhouse — the Agbajis drove down I-70.

Ochai turned to his father, Olofu, and, like a little kid who'd just met his hero, told him, "Dad, that was Coach Self! He just offered me a scholarship to play at Kansas."

Olofu got text messages after the offer came from other coaches who were recruiting Ochai. They said his son would never get any playing time. They were right, at first — Agbaji initially planned to redshirt as a freshman before joining the rotation in January. But then came the ascent.

Agbaji was a success story before this year. He led KU in scoring last year, forcing him to at least entertain the NBA Draft. But he'd still never really been a college star. Even though he averaged 14.1 ppg, Marcus Garrett was the face of the 2020-21 team. Agbaji wanted to use the draft process to see where he was and where working with Beckner could take him.

"He had no clue how good he could be, what it was going to take, like what first-rounders really do," Beckner says. "He was really honest and really open. He was really willing to get better, willing to take advice and hear stuff."

Beckner loves an underdog story. He started his coaching career at Weber State as an unpaid director of basketball operations. The next year Damian Lillard showed up on campus, and he became Lillard's guy, the two developing what they consider "the formula" to becoming a great player.

In Agbaji, Beckner saw more potential than he believed the player even saw in himself. He saw the body, the shot and the athleticism. He wanted to take his areas of strength from good to great, then identify areas of weakness: ball-handling, extending the range on his jump shot and being a relentless competitor.

Agbaji put in the work, staying after workouts to get in extra shots, then coming back at night for more shooting. But he had distractions that Beckner wanted to eliminate. Beckner called him one day and told him either do it the right way or go home. What he experienced in Phoenix was similar to what he says it's like entering the Jayhawks' program as a freshman. Self will snap at mistakes that seem small but are big to him and could prove costly in a game. "When you practice with that every single day, you build a habit of having that edge," Agbaji says. "And then once you get to the game, you can feel that trust because he puts you out there. And when you're out there, you know he trusts you because you've gone through all the practices. He's built you up for that moment to go play in the games."

Agbaji felt like a freshman again while training under Beckner. Fred Quartlebaum, Kansas' director of basketball operations, visited Agbaji in Phoenix in May and could tell his player was hurt that Beckner had questioned his preparation and his approach.

"In my mind, I was like, good," Quartlebaum says. "Good, because something good is about to happen on the other side. Because I knew what Phil was about."

Eventually, Agbaji sold out on the work and eliminated all distractions. He'd start every workout with a ball-handling series that Beckner created for Lillard. Agbaji had never been strong with his left hand, so he'd do the entire sequence and then repeat it again just with his left hand.

When Christian Braun hit the game-winning 3 at Oklahoma this season, Agbaji set him up with a left-handed drive. When Dajuan Harris made a last-second layup to beat Iowa State at Allen Fieldhouse, Agbaji drove left at his defender, opening up the seam for Harris to get to the basket.

"He would have never made two plays off his left hand in the past," Quartlebaum says.

A month into training, all the players in Beckner's camp were administered a wellness check. Beckner says some complained about sore legs and hips. Some needed massages. Agbaji felt great, except he said his right wrist was bothering him. A few days later, it swelled up. "Couldn't even shoot the ball," Agbaji says. "Couldn't flick it."

Beckner and his staff track everything, so they went to check the shooting numbers to see how much he'd shot.

"He blew away every pre-draft guy," Beckner says. "We had 15 dudes in Phoenix and some of them were on two-way contracts playing on NBA teams now. It wasn't even close how much he shot compared to everyone else."

Agbaji was shooting around 1,000 shots per day at game speed.

The wrist swelling coincided with a planned trip home for Memorial Day weekend, and a little rest was all he needed. On that trip, the Agbajis went to Lawrence to visit with Self. At that point, Self thought Agbaji was leaning toward staying in the draft. His parents thought the same. They believed Agbaji was skipping a step, trying to grow up too fast. Self relayed the feedback he'd received from NBA front offices, that Agbaji needed to be more aggressive.

"I left there thinking, OK, that's what we needed to hear," Erica Agbaji says.

Agbaji wanted to eliminate all doubt, so he started leaning toward a return to Kansas. Nonetheless, he returned to Phoenix and, with his wrist feeling better, went back to work.

Again and again, Becker worked Agbaji to the point where any reasonable person would quit. And time after time, Agbaji kept going.

"He tapped into something different mentally and physically that he had never done before," Beckner says.

Beckner was so impressed that he wanted to give Agbaji a sneak peek of his master class. So he kept dangling out the possibility of Agbaji joining him for a trip to Portland for a training session with Lillard.

Lillard is particular with who works out with him. In three years working for Beckner, Beamer says that Beckner had never invited any of the pre-draft players to work out with Lillard.

"If you're going to work with him, you've got to be about it," Beckner says. "I'm like, Dame, you got to give this kid a chance. I'm telling you, he's working really, really hard. He's like Phil, he's not messing up my workout. He's not getting in the way."

When it was finally time to go in mid-June, after the Trail Blazers had been eliminated from the playoffs, Lillard gave Beckner permission. Agbaji got the official invite.

"He was so excited," Olofu says, "It was like Christmas Day."

———————— ————————

One of Lillard's favorite quotes is "pit bulls and poodles can't be in the same kennel," and he wasn't about to let a poodle in his workout when Agbaji

arrived in Portland. So on Day 1, Lillard worked, and Agbaji watched.

Two weeks earlier Agbaji had watched Lillard drop 55 points in the playoffs against the Nuggets, and the thought crossed his mind, What else could Phil possibly say to Dame to make him better?

"It was weird watching them work out," Agbaji says. "It was not like how he talks to me. They wouldn't say anything. Phil would be like, 'OK, get your arm up.' Dame wouldn't say anything. He'd just do it."

Beckner worked on Lillard's shooting posture. Agbaji sat wide-eyed, thinking, He's shooting it great. How could he get better?

"It just put a lot of things in perspective as far as never being complacent," Agbaji says.

After Lillard's workout, the two traded places. Lillard watched from the sideline. Agbaji was nervous, feeling Lillard's eyes on him, and tried to be perfect. About 20 minutes in, as Agbaji worked on a dribble move, Lillard couldn't simply watch anymore. Agbaji was too stiff with the ball. Lillard walked over, put his arm around Agbaji and told him: "Breathe. Move. You want to glide here, dance with your feet."

Agbaji worked alongside Lillard for the remainder of the trip. Eventually, Lillard invited him over to his house to watch a Philadelphia-Atlanta playoff game before going to watch a high school basketball game. Agbaji peppered him with questions about what it takes to be successful in the NBA, especially as a rookie.

Lillard told him to learn the terms they use in the NBA, memorize scouting reports and be a professional. One of the key components to that, he told Agbaji, was a lesson Beckner had taught him: thank everyone.

"It goes a long way," Agbaji says. "It means something."

After every workout now, he thanks everyone in the gym. After the interview for this story, Agbaji thanked the author. And a couple days after Agbaji hit the shot to send the Texas Tech game to double overtime and scored a career-high 37 points against the Red Raiders, Lillard saw ESPN's Sean Farnham interview Agbaji on TV. He took a picture of his TV and sent him a text, telling Agbaji that he's getting better and he's proud of him.

Agbaji, wisely, responded with a thank you.

From one pit bull to another.

When Agbaji decided to pull his name out of the draft, it was quickly clear to his parents (and eventually his teammates) that he was a different man.

"Confidence," Erica says. "This is the first time I'd seen confidence."

Agbaji continued to work out at least six days a week. He'd go to his local trainer, Luther Glover, in the morning for four to five hours and then continue to get in extra shooting at night. Beckner would give him crap in their final days together that he wasn't going to keep working on what they'd worked on. A challenge. In August, Agbaji sent him a video. He'd propped his phone up on a court while going through a shooting drill.

"What can I do better?" he asked Beckner. "What do you think?"

"This kid gets it," Beckner says.

When Agbaji returned to Lawrence and met new teammates, he sat next to freshman Bobby Pettiford. He asked Pettiford about his summer, then started to tell Pettiford about his. Then Agbaji heard himself say out loud for the first time where he planned to go.

"You know what, Bobby?" he remembers saying. "I'm gonna be in the best shape that I can be this season. I'm just gonna keep working out, whether that be before practice, after practice, I'm going to push my body, just so I can put myself in the best position for the season to be good. For us to do something this year. I'm gonna lead this team. I'm telling you right now, this is what I'm going to do, and I'm going to do it. And if I don't do it and you see me not doing it, then hold me accountable. Tell me."

Agbaji has lived up to his word. It's the extra work that he's convinced makes all the difference.

"He's just so focused on what he wants," teammate Christian Braun says, "and it's obviously reflecting in how he's playing."

The tone was set on opening night against Michigan State when he scored what was then a career-high 29 points.

"Since day one when he got back, I think he wants to be the best player on the floor even when he's not the best player," Self says. "Sometimes when things are going bad, guys can kind of defer to somebody else that's going better. Ochai's still been the most aggressive guy, regardless if the ball's going in the hole or not."

Any tentativeness he had in his game is gone. Every move is made with force and conviction. In an open floor, he's one of the most feared players in the country.

"He hauls ass in transition, and he can stop on a dime and be on balance," Self says. "He's a very graceful player. He's athletic obviously, but he's almost added an element of a balance and gracefulness to his game."

Anyone can see that, but here's where Self really gets excited. Watch what happens when Agbaji doesn't get the ball in transition. He still, as Self puts it, hauls ass. Against Oklahoma State, he ran from one side of the floor to the other and took two defenders with him, leaving Braun wide open in front of KU's bench.

In the next huddle, Self told Agbaji he made that Braun 3 possible.

The respect level in the Big 12 has reached such a high level that teams have started to face-guard Agbaji. His response?

Coach, if they're going to play me like that, I need to be our best screener.

"He's thinking the game," Self says, "and how Kansas is better without thinking about him scoring points."

Self, of course, does not care about the points, but he does want the productivity to continue so Agbaji will have a chance to be an All-American. If nothing else, he wants him to win Big 12 Player of the Year.

"Because then he gets his number in the rafters," Self says, "and that would mean something to him."

Agbaji is not content, because the job is not finished. When he's asked if he sees himself as an All-American and lottery pick now, he says there's still work to be done. He'll only allow himself to evaluate what has already happened. So he's asked what his senior season would look like to date if he had never changed his ways.

"I would have had a better year than my junior year, but it wouldn't be anywhere near close to what I've done already," he says. "If I wouldn't have had that awakening over the summer, then I don't even think we are in contention to win the Big 12 this year. I don't think we're even top 10. I wouldn't have prepared myself for those moments, to win those (close games) like I did this year."

Before Agbaji left Phoenix, Beckner asked him if he'd seen anyone at Kansas work like he'd worked in the preceding months.

His response: no one.

"When you do things others don't do," Beckner tells him, "you get things others don't get."

So he works. The boring stuff, right? What you do when no one is watching, that's what matters. On Tuesday, game day, he shows up at 12:30 p.m. for an individual workout for 45 minutes. He goes from there to recharge his legs in Normatec boots, then to shootaround, then a meal and nap, then back to Allen Fieldhouse. He used to take the floor 65 minutes early with everyone else. Now he goes out 90 minutes before tip-off. He does his own work.

Day, after day, after day.

"That," he explains, "is just how it is now." ▄▄▄

```
SCORING      1   2  OT   T
Texas       33  24   6  63
Kansas      35  22  13  70
```

Staying In the Game

Senior Day Brings Mixed Results Ahead of Postseason

By CJ Moore

MARCH 5, 2022

K ansas lined all 20 of its Big 12 regular-season trophies on the Allen Fieldhouse floor after a 70-63 overtime win over Texas clinched a share of the conference title. It took five tables to hold all the trophies.

That's the same number of conference titles Bill Self has won as a coach — two each at Tulsa and Illinois and now 16 at Kansas — and the only college basketball legends with more are Phog Allen with 24 and Adolph Rupp with 28. Self has put himself in the conversation as one of the greatest college coaches ever, and it's hard to find anyone who can match his consistency in the regular season. Rupp won his conference 68 percent of the time. Self has coached in a conference for 25 seasons, so the math there is he wins the league he's in 80 percent of the time.

There's the *yeah*, but, of course.

Self has had all those great teams, but he's won only one NCAA championship.

That's explainable by what everyone witnessed on Saturday, not just in Kansas but in Durham as well. The pressure that comes with playing for a legend at a school like Kansas or Duke when a championship is on the line can mess with the mind. At Duke, it ruined a celebration. At Kansas, it nearly cost the Jayhawks a league title and ended an impressive streak that's now at 39 straight wins on Senior Day. "We played extra tight," Self said. "We couldn't buy a basket. Guys trying so hard, and the harder you try, the worse you play and shoot it."

66

The Jayhawks had the yips, much like some of Self's great teams have experienced in NCAA Tournament losses. Self has entered the tournament with arguably the best team five times (2008, 2010, 2011, 2016 and 2017), and only one of those teams won the title. That's the beauty (or curse?) of a single-elimination tournament.

And if you go back to all five of those teams' tourney runs, there's a game where the Jayhawks felt tight and just couldn't shoot like they normally would.

Kansas fans can rattle them off easily: Davidson, Northern Iowa, VCU, Villanova and Oregon. The Jayhawks survived only Davidson, with the coach on his knees as the buzzer sounded.

You might remember what happened next: Kansas played as free and easy in a Final Four game as you'll see, sprinting past Roy Williams and North Carolina. Then Mario Chalmers had the confidence to knock down one of the most pressure-packed shots in tourney history to give KU a chance to beat Memphis.

That history lesson is relevant because of what Kansas just went through in the span of three days. The Jayhawks knew they had to win their final two to achieve one of their goals; then you add the urgency to want to make Senior Day magical, and it's like trying to play basketball in a weighted jacket.

What Self will likely try to make the takeaway for his players is that they can win a game like that, and now he'll try to convince them the pressure is off. It's time to have fun.

It's not an easy sell, obviously, because they play at Kansas and know the terms. It is easier sometimes, however, when you're not the best team. That's the case this season. Self's team is good enough to make a Final Four appearance and maybe even win a national title if the bracket breaks right and Ochai Agbaji can go on a magical run, but the Jayhawks are not in the conversation as the best team in college hoops. And some of Self's teams like that have played better in March.

The hope in Lawrence is that because this team is much like the 2018 group, it, too, could catch fire and make the Final Four. The similarities are obvious. As in 2018, this team wins pretty with one of the best offenses in college basketball, led by one of the nation's best offensive weapons. That season it was Devonte' Graham. This season it's Agbaji.

Agbaji had his worst game as a senior against Texas, failing to reach double figures for the first time all season. He scored eight points on 1-of-11 shooting, not making a field goal until overtime. "He was just trying too hard," Self said.

The part Self liked was a team that's been one of his worst defensively showed something to him on that end.

"In order to have great years, you got to win ugly some," Self said. "We've been a team that was better offensively than defensively all year long. So for us to be better defensively than offensively, at least it shows us that we can do that."

It was a statement game, in particular, for KU's frontcourt of David McCormack and Jalen Wilson. In Austin, the Jayhawks struggled to contain Timmy Allen, who scored 24 points in the UT win. The Horns play a lot of isolation ball through Allen, and they tried to Saturday as well. Allen is the rare scorer who lives in the midrange and wins with leverage around the basket, getting his man to bite on pump fakes and finding small crevices to get off his shot.

Wilson and McCormack made sure to stay on the floor and keep their chests in front of Allen, and they held the UT star to 2-of-15 shooting.

McCormack playing with confidence on both ends is crucial to this team's success. He started the season struggling offensively and has been picked on defensively lately. Kansas has always been a much better team defensively with him on the floor, but the Big 12 has figured out the way to go at McCormack is in the middle third of the floor, using ball screens and isolation to get him to defend in space. With a nagging foot injury, he's struggled in those situations.

But in the past two games, McCormack is sliding his feet better. He was even allowed to switch some on ball screens against Texas, a strategy Self usually employs with the big fella only in the final seconds. McCormack and Wilson switched often successfully against Texas, and on the final possession of regulation, McCormack had the confidence to switch onto Texas guard Courtney Ramey. McCormack kept Ramey in front of him and forced the guard into a fadeaway jumper that he missed.

Wilson repeatedly won the matchup with Allen. "I think we picked up early that when you crowd him and give him pressure, that he's not the best ballhandler," Wilson said.

The one time Wilson didn't hold up like a brick wall, with about a minute left, McCormack saved him by flying in for a block. That's the kind of athleticism a hobbled McCormack hasn't always shown.

Self has also limited McCormack's minutes throughout the season, but that's probably out the window. McCormack played 36 minutes, and he hardly even noticed. "Dang," he said afterward when told the total, surprised he'd played that much. That's a good sign for the postseason that his legs can handle it.

Another good sign was KU's frontcourt carrying the offense on a day when Agbaji had nothing going. With UT face-guarding KU's star, the best option was to play through the post. Self wisely ran sets that took advantage of UT's defensive strategy, getting Agbaji on the weakside spot where the help defender would usually come from to fly at McCormack, giving him more space to operate.

McCormack missed some easy ones — Self said he was "pressing and trying too hard" as well — but even with McCormack struggling to make a few bunnies, those touches in tight for him were KU's most efficient offense. Wilson tipped in two of McCormack's misses, and McCormack got to the free-throw line five times. That's the spot where McCormack seems to be most at ease. He made all 10 of his free throws, has now made 16 in a row and finished at 84.2 percent at the line in conference play.

"They can't hack-a-Shaq," said McCormack, who scored a season-high 22 points. "I'm comfortable and I'm confident I'm gonna make it regardless."

It's good for Kansas to know there are options if Agbaji has another off night. Christian Braun (13 points), Wilson (17 points) and McCormack can carry the offense if need be, especially when so much attention is applied to Agbaji. If the Jayhawks collectively made a reasonable percentage of easy shots, they'd probably win easily in regulation.

But Saturday was proof their defense is capable of keeping them in a game when the ball just keeps rolling off the rim.

Now, the mental games start.

Self knows as much as any coach that the postseason is as much psychological as it is about the matchups. "In sports," he said, "you want to operate at a magic level where your energy and your focus and your adrenaline is all at a kind of crossroads to give you the best chance to play well."

That magic level is hard to reach. You have to appreciate the long-term success. That's why KU lined up those trophies and enjoyed the postgame festivities Saturday. No matter how this season ends, this team will always be able to say it won a championship. With this coach and this program, it's almost become the expectation, but it should still be celebrated. ▬▬▬

For the Love of the Game

Jalen Coleman-Lands and the Odyssey of 7-Year College Basketball Players

By Eamonn Brennan

MARCH 8, 2022

Traci Carter walked off the floor and into a hug. He had just had the best game of his abbreviated season, had been the best player in the gym on a night when the stakes, to anyone involved with Hartford men's basketball, couldn't have been higher. Hartford is transitioning its athletics programs to Division III next season. Carter and his coach, John Gallagher, and apparently everyone else on campus – save the administrators in charge of making the decision in the first place – are furious about it. There is a sense around the program that the only thing to do now is to rage against the dying of the light, to make as much noise and have as much success as possible, damn them all.

"Nothing is impossible," Carter says about the move to DIII; there is a part of him that thinks it could still be reversed. Maybe if Hartford wins the America East again. Maybe if it gets back to the tournament for the second straight year. Maybe. "It's about doing something legendary. It's about how people are going to remember you." So, yes, after his 21 points power Hartford past Albany in the conference tourney quarterfinal, Carter walks off the floor and his coach hugs him deeply, because what is happening with Hartford hoops is serious and emotionally fraught. To them, this is everything.

It is why Carter is still here, on the court in early March. It is why the 25-year-old left his job as a project engineer at a Hartford construction firm to utilize his last shred of eligibility and join his former team midseason – because he could see they were struggling, because they needed him. "He initiated it," Gallagher said. "I said, 'Well, if he wants to play, let him play.' And I remember thinking to myself: What a story this could be." On Sunday night, in the Albany win, that story added another page.

Carter used to hate basketball, you know. He thought the sport had betrayed him. He nearly quit. And now he's rushing out of retirement to stabilize Hartford's season and try to engineer one more March miracle. He is taking the ball for his guys in the pressure moments, making all the key free throws down the stretch, running the gym, all smiles and hugs, leading the Hawks, all of them years younger than he is, in the general direction of the NCAA Tournament.

It is his seventh season of college basketball.

Yes, seventh. Carter is the rarest of breeds: one of three seven-year players currently competing on men's Division I rosters. His story, like the others, is remarkable and winding, the product of injuries, disappointments, a pandemic and above all persistence. It is about dreams dashed and redefined.

In the coming weeks, all three careers will end. All three began their college careers in the final months of the Obama presidency. All three harbored aspirations of playing professional basketball. When those plans changed, they nonetheless found joy in the college game – and never more so than now.

Rick Stansbury remembers when the Camron Justice Idea was first discussed. It was the heart of the summer of 2021. The Western Kentucky staff was looking for guys who could scrimmage. A few former players were in town, professional players from overseas, and Stansbury's coaches were racking their brains for extra guys who could hold up to the competition. Stansbury asked his son, Noah, a walk-on, if he had any ideas.

"Get Cam," Noah said.

"I asked him, 'Cam? Can Cam still play?'" Stansbury said. "'Dad, he's been killing people out here.'"

This came as a total shock. Justice hadn't played organized basketball since the 2019-20 season ended. He had only recently arrived back in Bowling Green, Ky., to begin his planned year as a graduate assistant on Stansbury's staff – the very start, he hoped, of a nascent coaching career. Before that, though, Justice hadn't been around basketball at all. He had tried to begin the rest of his life, to start earning money and settling somewhere he and his fiancee, Kaylee, could plant roots. He moved to Huntington, W.Va., and took a job in plumbing sales. He figured he was probably done with basketball altogether.

His career, frankly, hadn't gone the way he'd hoped. Kentucky's 2014-15 Mr. Basketball his senior year of high school, Justice fielded high-major offers and settled on one from Vanderbilt, where – and, yes, this is how long ago this all was – Kevin Stallings was still the coach. As a freshman, Justice played in 26 games, averaged 3.4 points per game, and figured he was on his way to developing into a larger role as a Commodore, when Stallings left the job and Bryce Drew was hired. Justice suffered a sports hernia. He shut down his sophomore year after seven games, and transferred to IUPUI.

After sitting out the 2017-18 season, Justice averaged 18.6 points per game in 2018-19; he shot 245 3s and made 35 percent of them, and generally lived up to his high school promise. Stansbury – who had wanted Justice to come from Vanderbilt but didn't have a free scholarship to offer – finally brought him home. Justice had a degree from IUPUI and transferred as a graduate for what was supposed to be his last year of college hoops, in 2019-20, after which he hoped to find somewhere overseas to play. Instead, he spent most of the year banged up, first with a broken nose and then with back pain. The pandemic ended the season early and also canceled basically every international hoops league where Justice might have found a path to professionalism. The end of his career proved as maddening and unsatisfying as so much of the rest of it.

"Growing up in athletics, it's like, at the end, you always win or you lose," Justice said. "At the end of that season, there was just no closure."

Like so many in the pandemic, Justice felt isolated and adrift. He also knew he needed to start some semblance of a career. The plumbing sales work was fine, but maybe not super fulfilling. "I always tell people: I'm 25 and I'm back playing college basketball," Justice said. "That's about how it went."

But, of course, the initial plan for Justice's return for college basketball was to be a graduate assistant, and one primarily focused on working with Hilltoppers players academically. It was the one spot Stansbury had available. Justice jumped

at it. He wouldn't be drawing up the plays, but it was something.

And then came the pickup incident. Stansbury watched Justice play. Not only could he still get after it, he actually looked better than he had at any point when he was eligible at WKU. His body felt better; the year off from basketball activity had the effect of resetting his back pain and the nagging issues that had hampered him throughout his career. Now he just felt fresh. "I've always been confident in my ability to play at this level," Justice said. "I knew at the end of the COVID year that I had a chance to play as a pro. And I'm healthier now than I've been maybe in my whole career."

But there was something else, too. Whatever diminishing of Justice's love for the game that happened in 2020 was, by now, long gone. He and Kaylee had been willing to leave the day job and start down the GA path thanks in large part to Justice's renewed affection for hoops. Having

been away from it, he realized how much he loved it. Finally, now, he was playing like it.

"The game slowed down for him," Stansbury said. "The world slowed it down. The expectations go away. You wake up at 6 a.m. every day and go sit at your desk, that'll really slow things down. His body healed up, but the real world slowed him down and made him understand and appreciate this thing even more."

So, with a scholarship available and an everlasting need for perimeter shooting, Western Kentucky started working on his waiver. Justice thought it was a pretty ridiculous notion. Was the NCAA really going to let a 25-year-old dude who had played in five seasons of college basketball already, and then sat out for a whole year, get eligible again? It gradually became clear that the answer was yes.

Justice got the official news on Friday, Nov. 12. The rest of the Hilltoppers were in Asheville, N.C., for the 2021 Asheville Championship. Justice was in Bowling Green preparing for his wedding, which was scheduled for the next day. His phone was inundated with messages from team staff telling him a) his waiver was granted, true story and b) he needed to get to Asheville as soon as possible. Justice reminded everyone that he had to, you know, get married. So he did, and the day after his wedding, he and his wife woke up early and drove to Asheville. Justice played 17 minutes and scored three points in a 75-64 loss to South Carolina. He was back.

He's had an excellent season. It's probably the best year of his career, save the 2018-19 IUPUI breakout. In 2019-20, as he hobbled through injuries, Justice shot 32.6 percent from 3 and 45.2 percent from 2. His assist rate of 8.8 percent was vastly outdone by his 19.4 percent turnover rate. He ended the season with a 93.3 offensive rating – the worst in any full season of his career.

In 2021-22, Justice's offensive rating is 106.0. He is shooting 38.4 percent from 3 and 49 percent from 2; his assist rate is 18.3 percent. Last week, in an 86-72 win over Marshall, he scored 27 points on 9-of-9 from 2 and 3-of-6 from 3, plus four rebounds, four assists and three steals. He scored 25 in a home win over Louisville on Dec. 18. The Hilltoppers, 10-11 at the end of January, ended their season with nine wins in their last 10 games.

They received a double-bye in the Conference USA tournament, and will take the floor for the first time Thursday. Upending North Texas and/or UAB en route to the title and automatic bid will be easier said than done – but no other team in the league has as good a chance to do it.

Whatever happens, Justice will have more options available to him than he did two years ago. He might still give overseas pro ball a chance. He might start a coaching career. He'll figure that out in the offseason. For now, he's having a blast.

"This has just been – it's been so fun. It's been a journey," Justice said. "We've had our ups and downs. But more than anything, I'm just grateful."

Perhaps the most conventional of the seven-year guys – if there is anything conventional about playing for four schools in seven years – is Kansas guard Jalen Coleman-Lands.

His story is slightly more straightforward, though, again, this is all relative: We are talking, after all, about a 25-year-old still on intercollegiate athletics scholarship. Straightforward doesn't quite sum it up, though Coleman-Lands' view of it in hindsight is simple enough: "It's been great," he said. "Where I've been, the people that I've met, have all changed and molded me to become the man that I am now."

Coleman-Lands began his career at Illinois. He was a major recruit, a four-star top-40 player from La Lumiere School in the Class of 2015, who fielded offers from Indiana, Michigan, NC State, Notre Dame and UNLV. He signed on with John Groce in Champaign, the cornerstone of a top-15 recruiting class that was expected to resuscitate the already-flagging-in-year-four Groce era. That didn't pan out. Coleman-Lands was promising as a freshman, particularly as a spot-up perimeter shooter – he went 87-of-206 from 3, for 42.2 percent – when the Illini went 16-15. He slightly regressed as a sophomore, though the team improved, albeit not enough to make the tournament and save Groce's job.

Coleman-Lands, like so many players in this position, was faced with a choice: Wait around to see who Illinois hired, and take a gamble that the incoming coach would want him around, or take control of his own destiny right away. He chose the latter, and headed north to DePaul, where he could sit out a year and then join up with Dave Leitao. After sitting out the then-required transfer year, Coleman-Lands broke his left hand, ending his season after just nine games, for which he was eventually granted a medical hardship waiver.

Coleman-Lands returned in 2019-20 and played starters' minutes for a DePaul team that started promisingly (12-1 with three quality nonconference victories) and fell apart in Big East play (3-15, finishing the regular season 15-16). Then came COVID, and a chance for Coleman-Lands to get one more fresh start as a grad transfer to Iowa State. The year went about as badly as anyone could have imagined, despite some of the talent (Gonzaga's Rasir Bolton, Memphis's Tyler Harris are other guys who transferred from that team and are having success this season) on the floor. The Cyclones went 2-22 and 0-18 in league play, their only wins coming over Arkansas Pine Bluff and Jackson State. Steve Prohm was fired at the end of the season.

Coleman-Lands was facing the prospect of having had a seven-year college career without ever meaningfully winning in any one of those seasons. When Bill Self offered him a chance to join Kansas with his super senior year – even before he knew which of KU's star wings would return from the NBA Draft – he leaped at the chance. Last weekend, Kansas sealed a share of the Big 12 title, after Coleman-Lands nearly won the game at the buzzer. Self has raved all season about his super senior's work ethic, praising Coleman-Lands for grafting for the team despite foot injuries that have kept from playing at 100 percent.

Most importantly, the guard's path has long since changed his priorities. It is worth remembering that transferring in college basketball was, until not long ago, seen as slightly taboo; there was an idea that guys who transferred more than once must have something wrong with them. They couldn't commit, or they were spoiled, or whatever. Coleman-Lands' transience could have been a detriment to his academics. Instead, he has used it to his advantage, stretching out college long enough to earn multiple degrees, while currently working on another from Kansas in management information systems. He is also an aspiring entrepreneur: His "Athelites House" business is a start-up designed to give athletes in high school and college real-world lessons in how to budget and manage money. "It's a demographic that I've been a part of my whole life, as a student athlete," Coleman-Lands said. "It's a place where I can have

an impact." He is currently working on the core curriculum with local high school students in Lawrence and plans to launch a financial literacy app later in the year.

"I've learned so much about myself," Coleman-Lands said. "And it's given me time to figure out my passion outside of basketball."

Post-transfer portal, Coleman-Lands' career maybe reads slightly differently. But by being willing to move around, Coleman-Lands has fully explored the college experience. Now he is a Big 12 champion, with the potential for more. "To be able to compete for a national championship – it's something I've (technically) done, but I've never gone to the NCAA Tournament," Coleman-Lands said. "To actually be able to compete in it, to win our league, these are a lot of collegiate milestones that I haven't had a chance to be a part of, that this extra year has given me."

Traci Carter had reluctantly agreed to take one more meeting with one more coach. He didn't want to go. All he had ever wanted to do was play basketball. Now he hated it. He just wanted to be done.

Carter had grown up in challenging circumstances in Philadelphia. His mother struggled with drug addiction. He was raised by his grandmother with five of his six siblings. Basketball was his refuge, the thing that gave him a window outside his current environment, what got him out of the city (and some teenage decisions) to Life Center Academy in New Jersey, where he excelled. A four-star guard, he received offers from Xavier, Cincinnati, UConn, Creighton and Marquette. He chose Marquette. His freshman season under Steve Wojciechowski was promising: He played in 33 games, started 19, and finished sixth in the conference in assists, just 16 behind Villanova legend Ryan Arcidiacono. Carter struggled with his shot and turned the ball over too often, but these are not uncommon hiccups for freshman guards playing big minutes at the high-major level.

Carter's plan was simple: Come back to Marquette, iron out the wrinkles, make the leap, get to the NBA, and take care of his family and friends for the rest of their lives. Easy.

Then, four games into his sophomore season, Wojciechowski called Carter in for a meeting. From here on out, freshman guard Markus Howard was going to start in Carter's place. Carter became unstuck. "It shocked my world," he said. "You have to understand, where I come from, there's only a couple of ways to make it out of there. As a kid that's what you think, anyway. I have friends that are dying. His decision just crushed my whole world. I became depressed without even knowing I was depressed."

Carter, reeling, decided to transfer after just eight games. He didn't have a destination in mind. "I didn't have anywhere to go," he said. "I just wanted to leave." He admits now the decision-making process wasn't the most reasonable, but he panicked. For him more than most, basketball felt like life and death, and he felt he had been left to fend for himself. "My way of making it was gone," he said.

Carter went home and took online classes. His mentor, current La Salle assistant coach and Philly hoops institution Donnie Carr, then an assistant at Hartford, put Carter up while he figured things out. After half a year away from the game, Carter transferred to La Salle, under coach John Giannini, where he would work out for a year and be eligible at the start of the 2018-19 season. Instead, Carter tore the meniscus in his knee for the third time, and had the third knee surgery of his young career. Most of his off year was spent recovering from injury. Then, Giannini was fired, and La Salle hired former Villanova assistant Ashley Howard.

"That was one of the worst times of my life," said Carter, who led the team in assists and steals. "From a basketball standpoint. From a life standpoint. Me and Ash just did not get along there. It was confusing. It was so disheartening. It

wasn't fun anymore. It made me lose my passion." Carter was also back in Philadelphia, back in a "negative environment," as he called it, and beginning to feel desperate.

"It was a nightmare," Carter said. "The whole time that year at La Salle, in my head, I said: Let me just get through this year, and I ain't never playing basketball again."

Carter's career could have ended there. It would have, if not for Carr, who encouraged Carter to talk to some coaches. Carter reluctantly agreed. He and Carr went to dinner with Gallagher. Carter, going through the polite job-interview motions, dutifully asked what Gallagher thought he needed to improve in his game.

"You need to dream again," Gallagher said.

Both men recall this story, this statement, verbatim. "That was so profound to me at that time in my life," Carter said.

"His eyes lit up," Gallagher said. The coach, friends with Carr and familiar with Carter's struggles, could see immediately he had struck a nerve. "It was like, Traci, man, if you don't have that little boy feeling when you go into a gym, you don't have that energy, then you're working from a place of obligation. Sometimes when you get high-major players, because I've had a few of them, they work out of obligation. That's why they fail."

Just like that, Carter fit in. It clicked. He found himself at home. Gallagher's relentless positivity and intentional fostering of a tight community bond – he calls Hartford hoops and its fans "The Neighborhood," mentioned in every interview and loudly emblazoned at the Hawks' home gym – was exactly what the guard needed. One of his best friends and former high school teammates, Malik Ellison, joined him at Hartford soon after. Carter also started going to therapy, where he learned that he had been depressed, and where he began to understand how to work through the trauma of his childhood and the disappointments of his career.

In 2019-20, Carter – a member of the league's honor roll with a 3.5 GPA – and Ellison led Hartford to the America East championship game, one win away from the school's first NCAA Tournament, just before the season was canceled. In 2020-21, Carter returned, scored 20, 22 and 19 points in three straight games at the America East tournament, and led the Hawks to the first NCAA Tournament in program history. "He's the most important player in the history of Hartford basketball," Gallagher said.

Carter's redemptive success could have been derailed by grief. In July 2020, he learned that his brother, Semaj Carter, had been shot and killed. Traci Carter insists his brother was the smartest in the family but fell victim to his environment – the same environment Carter had been desperate to escape. Carter felt guilty; if he was in the NBA, would Semaj still be alive? But with his Hartford support structure around him, with his own self-understanding, he was able to process his grief and turn it into something more – founding a boys camp, Anchors Camp, for young men to have an outdoor experience of self-discovery at a farm in upstate New York. "The camp is so special," Carter said. "It's there for the people that I was trying to make it out for."

With the tournament putting a lovely cap on a long career, Carter thought his actual hoops life was over. He moved on to running his camp nonprofit – it will expand to two cities in the coming summer, when he moves into the role full-time – and a day job as an engineer at FIP Construction in Farmington, Conn.

Then he saw how much Hartford was struggling at the start of the 2021-22 season, its last in Division I. The Hawks lost their first seven games. Carter got in touch and just threw it out there: He still had that extra year of eligibility. Would the coaches like him back? Would the rest of the team be cool with it? Could he be of use? Yes, yes and yes.

Just like that, the guy who wanted to quit college basketball found a way – an extremely rare way – to keep doing it for a seventh straight year. "It's

ironic," Carter said. "But my whole thing now is to live life fully, in the best possible way, through love." Love of basketball included.

The regular season was a way for Carter to get back into playing shape. "Everything, for us, comes down to three days in March," Gallagher said. "March 6 is when our season starts. And that's where Traci is going to help us." Carter already led Hartford through the first win-or-go-home outing against Albany on Sunday afternoon. Next up is UMBC on Wednesday in Baltimore. At times he moves like a 25-year-old who has had three knee surgeries – he has not shot the ball well inside the arc this season, where his legs don't help him – but the outside shot is falling, and his game is dripping with experience and savvy.

He used to hope that he could get to the NBA, get money, make it out. The plan derailed, but not to his detriment. The plan now is to win two more games in the A-East, to tell hiws story and Hartford's, to see what happens from there. It has been a long, winding path from Philly to The Neighborhood, from boy to man. After seven years, Carter – like Justice and Coleman-Lands – has one more March to become legend. ▬▬▬

Big 12 Tournament

SCORING	1	2	T
Texas Tech	36	29	65
Kansas	37	37	74

'This is What You Came Here For'

Remy Martin Brings the Extra Element in Big 12 Championship Win

By CJ Moore

MARCH 12, 2022

Christian Braun dapped up Remy Martin on the floor at T-Mobile Center in the final moments of a 74-65 Big 12 tournament championship win for Kansas and told Martin, "This is what you came here for."

Martin then headed across the court and was met by Kansas coach Bill Self, who for a moment put his right arm around the fifth-year point guard and told him "good job."

The bouncer had decided to let him in. Welcome to the party, Mr. Martin.

Martin was part of the machine again over the final two days in Kansas City. He made an impact. A good one. It was a wonder if he'd ever experience that again. The journey to get here, everyone knows now, has had its twists and potholes.

Martin injured his knee all the way back on Dec. 29. Before then, the experiment was mostly working. KU was better with Martin than without. But since then, he's been more of an outsider than an integral part of the team. Heck, sometimes he's even been a bit of a distraction.

That's the danger, of course, of hitting the transfer portal to try to find a quick fix. That's what Self was doing after last spring. Self went looking for a point guard who could score and give his offense life again. A year ago the Jayhawks often sputtered offensively if things didn't go exactly according to plan. The USC blowout loss in the second round was the alarm bell. KU needed more speed and more scoring. Self has always liked to have a little guard who can go get a bucket when a possession fell apart, and on tape, it was apparent Martin was capable.

The thing is that Self also expects a lot out of his point guards. His trust is not easily won. Sometimes it takes years before what Self wants and his point guard gives fully align.

When Martin is on the floor, he's constantly looking over at Self. Sometimes it's for a play call, but often it's the look of a son seeking his father's approval.

Am I doing it right? What can I do better?

"He wants to do the right things," KU assistant coach Norm Roberts said of Martin. "He always does."

Self hasn't had a ton of patience, because that's how he wins so much. He gets players to execute what he wants, and if you cannot do so, then he'll find someone who can. That someone is point guard Dajuan Harris, who isn't flashy but is reliable.

Harris was in foul trouble against Texas Tech, and the opportunity was there for Martin to prove himself in a game that really mattered. Texas Tech's defense demands improvisation. Martin was playing well in the first half, scoring the ball and mostly in the right spots defensively. Then in the final minute before halftime when Self took a timeout to set up a two-for-one, the play was not executed as designed, and Martin went off script, using a ball screen to pull up for a long jumper at the top of the key that he buried.

"He is a guy that gives us an extra element, that can kind of go get his own a little bit," Self said, "that can allow you to have good possessions even though you really don't run good stuff."

That's what has to happen sometimes in the NCAA Tournament. But for Martin to be part of that plan, simply making a few shots wasn't going to earn Self's trust. But what he did in the second half might.

With six minutes left and the game still in doubt, Texas Tech's Clarence Nadolny knocked the ball away from David McCormack and was just about to pick it up when Martin stuck his nose in and tapped it up to McCormack. The hustle play generated two points for Kansas — McCormack made two free throws after getting fouled on a dunk attempt — and it probably kept Martin on the floor.

Instead of going back to Harris, like Self typically would, the coach kept riding Martin. The point guard added to his trust bank a few minutes later when following a Braun bucket, Martin bolted in front of Texas Tech guard Adonis Arms, forcing Kevin Obanor to step over the end line. The violation gave the ball back to Kansas, Jalen Wilson scored and a four-point lead had quickly been stretched to eight. That play was the dagger.

Martin loved it, of course, because the crowd loved it. That's his fuel. It's no wonder that he just didn't look like himself in his final year at Arizona State. Martin is best with an audience, and the pandemic and the losing were draining. It's part of why he went looking for a better ending to his college career.

This is what he had in mind, and he was feeling himself Saturday, pumping his fist repeatedly, revving up the crowd. The louder they got, the faster he flew.

"These guys can tell ya, I think that's the quickest we've seen him look in two months," Self said with Ochai Agbaji and Braun both nodding in agreement. "I mean he looked like a different guy health-wise. And so I do think it gives us an additional element."

Martin, standing on the floor afterward as the celebration went on around him, admitted that he had doubts the last few months if this day would ever come. "Every time I would get a little bit healthier, I would reinjure it," he said. "Now I feel back. I feel normal."

It was a process, obviously. Martin was going to have to prove himself again, especially after looking unreliable in the short spurts he's played in recent weeks. He still makes some decisions that drive Self crazy. But if he keeps those to a minimum and leans on his speed and energy, then he's going to get a chance. In Kansas City, Self altered his substitution patterns to make sure there were minutes for Martin and fellow backup guard Joseph Yesufu, the other speedster Self brought in to address what last year's team lacked.

A lot has changed since last March. Agbaji turned into an All-American. KU's offense hasn't really needed much scoring out of its point guards. It has become one of the nation's best offenses without it. The returners are the reason Kansas will find itself on the No. 1 seed line Sunday.

But there may come a time in the next few weeks when the plan goes to mush and Self needs Martin to provide some more improvisation. He signed him so he'd have every bullet he needed to get to a

Final Four, and Martin came to Kansas to play on those stages.

This is what you came here for.

The point guard emerged from the celebratory postgame locker room Saturday sporting a Big 12 champions hat with a piece of the net stuck in the back. He also rocked a pair of sunglasses. A bold look for a bold dude. A sign that his swagger has fully returned.

Someone asked Martin if he'd ever cut down a net before.

"Never cut nets," he told the crowd around him. "And I'm planning to cut a couple more." ▬▬

'I've Never Seen a Whole Team Cry'

The Ecstasy, Agony of '97 Kansas, the Best-Ever Team to Miss the Final Four

By CJ Moore

MARCH 15, 2022

On the day of his Hall of Fame induction in 2007, Roy Williams jotted down notes for his speech, because he thought he'd have a better chance of getting through it without tears if he could read off a piece of paper. One thing Williams decided it was important to do that day was apologize to his 1996-97 Kansas team.

Those Jayhawks, who finished 34-2 and lost to eventual national champion Arizona in the Sweet 16, are considered one of the greatest teams of all time to not win a national title.

Williams made it seven minutes into his speech — then it was time to talk about 1997. As soon as he hit the word "failed," he felt that lump in his throat.

"It's still the biggest regret I had in my coaching career," Williams says now.

It was near the end of the heyday of college hoops, when players stayed until graduation and were willing to put off millions. Jacque Vaughn, one of four first-rounders on that roster, had returned for his senior year. Paul Pierce, a sophomore swingman, would go on to become a Hall of Famer. Raef LaFrentz, another eventual lottery pick, led the team in scoring and was a two-time first-team All-American. Vaughn and Jerod Haase, the starting backcourt and now coaches, were Academic All-Americans.

"I still feel like I let that team down," Williams says. "It was the most fun team, and the easiest team to coach I've ever had."

It was, in many ways, the perfect college team.

Williams kept an airline directory on the corner of his desk, and he'd memorized every flight that went to Los Angeles International Airport and when the red-eyes returned to Kansas City. "He knew those fights like a New Yorker would know the train schedule back to Long Island," says Matt Doherty, who was an assistant at Kansas from 1992 to 1999.

When Williams arrived at Kansas, he'd wanted to recruit nationally. But he quickly learned the competition was fierce on the East Coast, where he was competing with the ACC, Big Ten, Big East and SEC schools. On the West Coast, however, it was mostly just Pac-10 schools. "There were so many players," Williams says, "and they couldn't all go to UCLA or Arizona."

Williams also wisely did the math that the two-hour time difference would benefit KU. The Jayhawks were often playing on ESPN during dinner time on the West Coast. KU had essentially been in their living rooms for years. He decided to forget about the East Coast, especially after his efforts failed in trying to land Felipe Lopez out of New York City. He would travel to Los Angeles every spring and fall weekend.

His first recruit, Adonis Jordan, lived in Reseda, Calif., a neighborhood in the San Fernando Valley. When Jordan graduated in 1993, Williams found the ideal replacement in Jacque Vaughn out of Pasadena. The challenge in those pre-cell phone days was staying in contact. Vaughn was a serious student whose goal was to be high school valedictorian. Every day he'd go home, grab a snack and then head to the library, where there were no distractions. "He was hard to get to," Williams says, "probably harder to get to than any player I ever successfully recruited."

Williams called every night, and the way he won, as it often was, was in the living room. He sold Vaughn's mom on Kansas, emphasizing that education and developing young men was part of the plan.

His ability to come across as a father figure also helped him land Scot Pollard, a 6-foot-11 center out of San Diego. Pollard lost his father when he was 16 and wanted someone who could fill that void.

"I knew going to college I was going to have to respect the man that I was going to go play for," Pollard says. "Had to be somebody that if I started every game and played every minute, I would respect his decisions, and if I didn't play any minutes and didn't play any games, I'd still respect his decisions."

The two coaches who Pollard felt fit what he was looking for were Williams and Arizona coach Lute Olson. In the fall of 1996, he visited Tucson and committed but didn't tell the Kansas coaches. The next weekend he attended KU's annual "Late Night with Roy Williams."

"Seventeen-thousand people don't go indoors in San Diego at any time for anything," Pollard said. "And walking in there and seeing that just for a practice, I was just blown away."

Williams promised Pollard he wouldn't eat any desserts until Pollard made his decision. It was cheesy, sure. But it was a symbol to Pollard that Williams was invested. So after Late Night, Pollard asked one of the managers to go buy a German chocolate cake — Williams' favorite — and Pollard gave it to Williams. "Well, you know I can't eat this until you decide," Williams told Pollard. Pollard said he was coming to Kansas, and Williams enjoyed the cake.

Also part of that class was Jerod Haase, who played alongside Jason Kidd in the Cal backcourt as a freshman. When Kansas beat California in the Sweet 16 in 1993, Haase had already decided to leave Cal, and he'd learned enough about Kansas to know that was a place he'd like to play. A visit to the KU locker room after losing to the Jayhawks cemented his stance.

With his future backcourt in place and a defensive-first center in Pollard, Williams knew he needed

a scoring big man. He found one in the summer of 1992 at a grassroots tournament in Winston Salem, N.C. Eddie Fogler, who worked alongside Williams as an assistant at North Carolina, ran into Williams between games and told him he'd just watched a player that had Kansas written all over him. "Who the dickens is that?" Williams asked. It was Raef LaFrentz. Three hours later, Williams watched LaFrentz, a quiet, coach's son from Monona, Iowa, and he was blown away. For the next two years, he called LaFrentz every Sunday night at 9:30. LaFrentz would end up ranked the No. 2 prospect in the 1994 class, according to Bob Gibbons, the renowned recruiting expert at the time, and Williams beat out the Iowa schools for the gifted LaFrentz.

A few months later, then-assistant coach Steve Robinson discovered Paul Pierce at a fall league in Los Angeles. All Williams needed to complete the perfect starting five was a small forward. Williams says he believes over the next three years he watched Pierce more than any other coach through his frequent trips to LA — Pierce was from Inglewood. KU was the only school that wasn't out West that recruited Pierce, who was also considering UCLA, USC, Cal, Oregon, Arizona and UNLV.

Pierce visited KU over Thanksgiving break for the season opener in 1994 against San Diego. The students were gone, but the Fieldhouse was still packed.

"I'd never seen a crowd like that," Pierce says. "There were people camping out for the game. I'd never seen that. I didn't understand it until I was in it. You could watch it on TV, but to actually be in it, when I sat in that crowd and watched that game, I was like, 'I'm coming here.'"

When it was time for Pierce to make his decision, Williams cut a square piece of cardboard into five pieces. He mailed the four corners to Pierce, then two days later sent the middle piece with a picture of Pierce glued to it and a message that read Pierce was the missing piece.

Pierce committed, and the puzzle was complete.

Vaughn was the first freshman at Kansas to start a season opener since Danny Manning in 1984-85. Haase locked himself into the starting spot alongside Vaughn after going home to Tahoe between his redshirt season and what would be his redshirt sophomore year, hiking and running through the mountains and returning in incredible shape.

"When he came back all ripped up," Pollard says, "we would say, 'Jerod, you need to put your shirt on before you go in public, because if you walk around like that, you're not going to be able to get anywhere.'"

Haase led the Jayhawks in scoring during the 1994-95 season, averaging 15 points per game. LaFrentz, like Vaughn the year before, started every game as a freshman. Pollard and senior Greg Ostertag split the minutes at center, with Pollard averaging 10.2 points coming off the bench. The Jayhawks won the Big Eight and were a No. 1 seed, eventually losing in the Sweet 16 to Virginia and finishing 25-6. The next year with Pierce joining the lineup, they were even better, winning the Big Eight again. They ranked in the top five the entire season, but their season ended on a cold-shooting night in Denver in the Elite Eight against Syracuse's zone defense. They went 4-of-25 from 3 and were upset 60-57.

"It's not good enough. It's not good enough for Coach Williams," Haase told the Kansas City Star. "He deserves better."

KU's starting five were eligible to return, but Vaughn had a decision to make. "I have two dreams," he said after the loss. "A dream of playing in the NBA and a dream of going to the Final Four and winning the championship. Now I'm just going to think about this a lot and leave it in the hands of God."

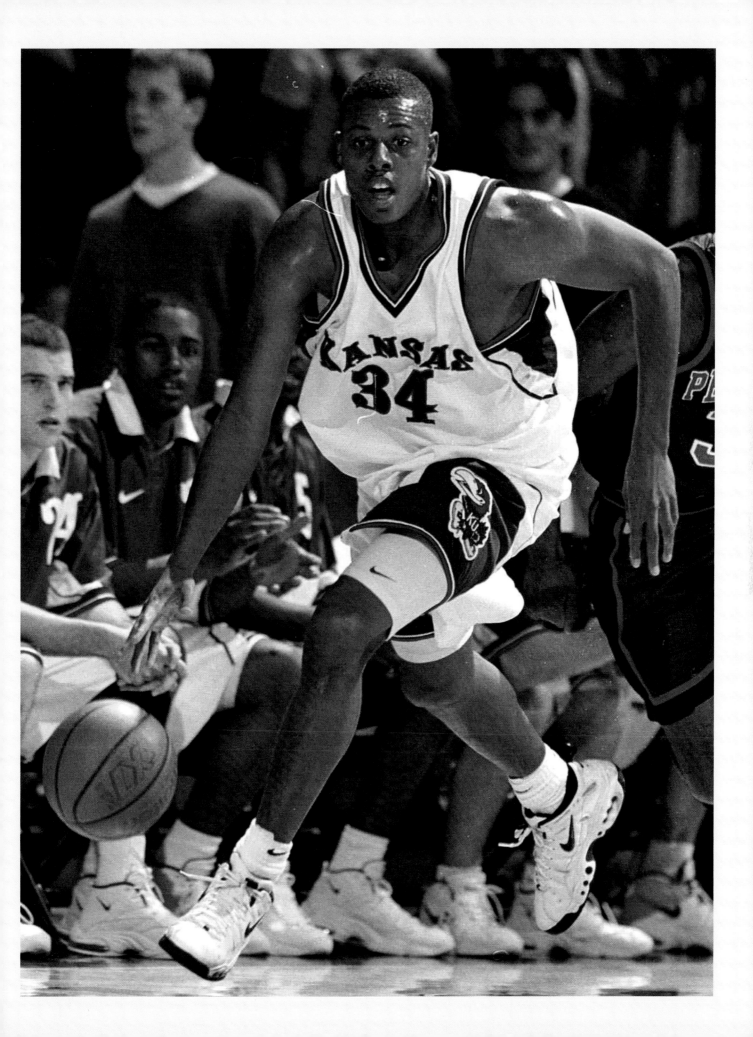

"That was on all of our minds," Pollard says. "I mean everybody on the team was like, 'We can be the best team in the country next year' — which we ended up being — but obviously it depends on if Jacque's going or staying."

As the point guard contemplated the choice, Williams asked Vaughn to go to church with him.

The sermon was on big life decisions. Vaughn felt like it spoke to him, and that night he called and told Williams he wanted to stay in school and try to win a championship.

"We thought, this is our year," Pierce says. "That's the expectation at Kansas. You've got to expect 'this is your year' every year. We felt like we could win a national championship my freshman year, but even more so the next year with everyone returning, it was just like, this has got to be it."

In the summer of 1996, Pierce established himself as the most talented player in the program. He was 17 when he enrolled at Kansas, and he'd arrived "all elbows and knees," Pollard says. His teammates nicknamed him "Bambi."

"We could tell greatness was coming," Pollard adds. "We knew it. We could see it."

Pierce grew into his body between his freshman and sophomore years, and he was obsessed with getting better. He'd play pickup ball with whomever, wherever. He was competitive, too. When Shane Battier came for a visit that fall, he was scheduled to play a pickup game at Allen Fieldhouse with the team.

Battier always wore a headband in high school, so the Jayhawks rocked headbands to make Battier feel good. Pierce wore the headband, but he didn't exactly help the cause.

"Paul Pierce just destroyed this dude," walk-on guard Terry Nooner says. "Like, he wouldn't even let him get his shots off. Every time he shot the ball, he blocked his shot. Scored on him like every single time."

The Jayhawks knew they were about to destroy college basketball, then doubt crept in for the first time.

During a pickup game inside the Fieldhouse on Sept. 10, Vaughn fell on his right wrist. He jogged out of the gym and went straight to the trainer. X-rays showed ligament damage that would require surgery, and the feeling of invincibility was gone, at least temporarily.

"I would say that there was definitely some apprehension," says Ryan Robertson, Vaughn's replacement in the lineup.

"Everything we did centered around Jacque," Pierce says. "He was the engine that made us go, and so that was a huge concern."

In the mid-90s in Kansas, every little kid in Kansas wanted to be Jacque Vaughn. You could walk into any gym in the state those days and probably find a boy with a rubber band around his wrist, like Vaughn used to wear, snapping it anytime he made a mistake.

He wrote poetry. He was always the best-dressed. Sports Illustrated's Jack McCallum set out to find the perfect student-athlete in 1995 and landed in Lawrence. "Well," Williams said at the time, "you found him."

Vaughn was so organized that he'd plan out every minute of his day. Right down to when he would call home — midnight, so he could take advantage of the long-distance rates.

His teammates didn't just look up to him; they worshiped him.

On the day of his surgery at KU Medical Center, a nurse came in to say he had some teammates there to see him. "How many?" Williams asked.

"I think it's the whole team," the nurse said. "Maybe more than one team."

Vaughn and Williams went out to the waiting room, and every member of the Jayhawks was there. "I still think to this day that's the most amazing confirmation of what a great leader he was and how his teammates cared," Williams says.

Robertson, meanwhile, was anxious about trying to fill in for not just any All-American, but that one. Robertson was 6-5 and more of a shooting guard than a point guard. He was talented — a McDonald's All-American — but he hadn't started a collegiate game.

On the way to the Maui Invitational, Kansas opened the season at Santa Clara. Robertson had a decent line — 11 points, two assists and two turnovers — but he fouled out in 28 minutes in a 76-64 Jayhawks win.

"He's got to stop the silly reach-in fouls," Williams said after. "I really don't need him sitting over here with me."

The Jayhawks responded in Maui, beating LSU, California and Virginia by an average of 21.3 points per game. LaFrentz established himself as an All-America caliber player in Maui, winning tourney MVP honors. Pollard and Haase also made the tournament team, and Pierce did not, despite scoring 27 points in the final against Virginia. That's one he's held onto for 25 years. "I felt slighted," Pierce says.

That same week, No. 1 Cincinnati lost a two-point game to Xavier, meaning the Jayhawks would be the new No. 1. That same day a new Sports Illustrated hit newsstands with Cincinnati star Danny Fortson shirtless on the cover. The Bearcats were SI's preseason No. 1 and the pick to win the national title.

Two days later, they'd get to settle it on the court at the United Center.

That SI story captured how Cincinnati was essentially the polar opposite of Kansas. The Bearcats had rap sheets. and Bob Huggins had a poor record for graduating players. The front cover suggested Cincinnati could dominate everyone in the weight room, and the KU players had heard everyone on Cincy's team could bench press at least 300 pounds. The Jayhawks joked amongst themselves that basketball games weren't won in the weight room.

Fortson also said there weren't many players at "those big-name schools" who were tough enough to play in their program, which was perceived as a dig at the clean-cut boys ranked right behind them. "They couldn't play here," he said. "Men come through here."

The Bearcats intimidated, and the Jayhawks allowed the stereotype to play out for a half. Cincinnati grabbed 14 offensive rebounds in the first 20 minutes and led 35-23.

"They came out strong-arming us, and we were playing soft," Nooner says. "We go into the halftime, and Coach Williams comes in and goes crazy. He smashes the whiteboard. He gets in front of everyone's face nose to nose and says, 'You were scared. And I knew y'all were scared when you were talking about how much they bench-pressed.'"

His speech worked. Pierce took over, scoring 15 points in the second half, and KU blew past the Bearcats to win 72-65.

"I hate when people call us a soft basketball team," Williams said. "I don't think we're a soft basketball team. But I told them we played soft basketball."

Three days later, Kansas visited Pauley Pavilion and ran UCLA off the floor in a 96-83 win. Robertson had 11 assists, and he remembers saying that Williams had handed him the keys to a Ferrari. "It was my job to just drive the car around and not scratch it up," he says.

Dreams of an undefeated season started to become part of the conversation. In the next day's Kansas City Star, sports columnist Jason Whitlock wrote:

"Don't blame me for placing this extra burden on Coach Roy Williams and his No. 1-ranked Kansas Jayhawks. CBS college basketball broadcaster Billy Packer raised the possibility first.

"Kansas is built to run the table, wipe the plate clean, kick booty all year."

When asked if the players felt like it was a real possibility, Pollard says now, "Absolutely."

Vaughn returned for the 11th game, and the Jayhawks kept rolling. Their first close call was on the road at Kansas State, where they shot 28.8 percent. They won 62-59 by holding the Wildcats to 32.8 percent shooting and outscoring them by 10 at the free-throw line.

"I remember going to the locker room and (KU assistant coach) Joe Holladay came up behind me and said, 'Don't be so mad. It's still a win,'" Williams remembers. "I told him, 'I'm happy. You got to win ugly sometimes.'"

The offense, the tempo and crazy runs are what most fans remember about that team, but the defense made it all possible.

"Everything started with our defense," Pierce says. "We took on Roy's personality, man, because he was intense. You looked over at him on the sideline, and you were just fired up."

The Jayhawks played a style similar to some of the best defenses in college today, trying to keep the ball out of the middle of the floor and forcing it baseline toward Pollard and LaFrentz.

"They were the best defensive team I ever coached," Williams says. "You had Raef and Scot who could block shots. Paul could slide his feet better than anybody, and Jacque and Jerod were the best tandem guards defensively I ever coached."

After the trip to Manhattan, the Jayhawks had their first Big 12 meeting with No. 22 Texas. "Tom Penders was talking about how they're the 'Running Horns,' and they were going to come in and run everybody out of the gym," Doherty says. "We blew their doors off, and Coach Williams was shocked that they were walking the ball up the court."

KU did smoke Texas, 86-61, but the good times did not last. The next Saturday at Baylor, Pollard rolled his ankle, hearing a pop.

"I was pissed," Pollard says. "I walked off the court and walked to the locker room, and I knew I was gonna have to sit out awhile because I knew that was a bad ankle sprain. And like an idiot, I just taped it up and played the next game, because I didn't want us to lose because we were undefeated."

Two days later, Kansas played No. 8 Iowa State on Big Monday. Pollard was extra motivated to play because the Cyclones had a NBA prospect at center in Kelvin Cato, and he wanted to prove he was an NBA-caliber player as well. He won the battle — going for 10 points and seven boards while Cato fouled out with seven points and two boards — and KU won the game, 80-67, but Pollard paid for playing. The next day he was walking back to the Jayhawker Towers from class when he heard a pop. Doctors later told him that by wrapping his ankle so tight the pressure went to his forefoot and weakened the metatarsal bones. His third metatarsal snapped, and the fourth one had a stress fracture.

Without Pollard, the Jayhawks beat UConn and Texas A&M, then had to travel to No. 18 Colorado. The Buffaloes were off to a 6-0 start in league play and ranked for the first time in 30 years.

They were led by star sophomore guard Chauncey Billups, who had been recruited by KU. At the time, Kansas had one scholarship left and was after both Billups and Pierce, and the story goes that Pierce committed before Billups could ever visit. Billups nearly got his revenge, banging six 3s in the second half and helping the Buffs take a one-point lead, 64-63, with five minutes left.

"I only saw Jacque get in trouble one time, and that was that game at Colorado," Nooner says. "Chauncey went off, and Jacque was trying to go back at him. Coach called a timeout and said, 'This is Kansas versus Colorado, not Jacque versus Chauncey!'"

KU finished on a 14-3 run to win 77-68.

The Jayhawks got pushed again the next weekend at home against Nebraska, the game surprisingly going to overtime tied at 60. LaFrentz, the team's leading scorer, had just nine points in regulation. In overtime, he told his teammates, "Give me the damn ball!"

He scored 10 of KU's first 12 in OT to lead the Jayhawks to an 82-77 win that put the Jayhawks at 22-0, a school record for most wins to start a season.

Three days later, Kansas was pushed to overtime again at Missouri. Mizzou led by three in the final seconds of regulation and tried to foul up three. Vaughn made the first free throw, then intentionally missed, and LaFrentz rebounded the miss and scored to send the game to overtime. LaFrentz again nearly carried the Jayhawks to a win, scoring 12 of his 26 points in the extra 10 minutes. No team led by more than three in the two overtimes. With the score tied at 94, the Tigers held the ball for the final shot. KU went to its run-and-jump trapping defense. Mizzou wing Tyron Lee ended up with the ball on the left wing, and when Vaughn went to trap, he knocked it loose. The ball squirted behind Vaughn into the hands of Mizzou senior Corey Tate, who buried a 16-footer with 5.6 seconds. LaFrentz missed a 3 at the buzzer, and KU's undefeated dream ended in Columbia.

"I'm not going to 'Uncle Rico' it," Pollard says, "but I was the best player at my position, and that's why I started. So I would like to think that if I had played against that Missouri team in that game we would have won."

KU had to play one more game without Pollard at No. 6 Iowa State that Sunday, Feb. 9, and its 69-62 win kept the Jayhawks at No. 1 in the polls.

With Pollard back, they looked unbeatable again, beating Oklahoma State 104-72 and then No. 15 Colorado 114-74.

"When we'd get up against those teams, especially the teams we were not supposed to blow out, that's when we really wanted to put the gas on," Pollard says. "Because it was like, we're better than you and we're going to embarrass you."

KU's depth helped turn some of those games ugly. Robertson, Thomas, B.J. Williams and T.J. Pugh could have started on most teams in the league. "If you were subbed out, your guy would go in and get 10 points," Pollard says. "It was like, oh, man, I gotta get back in there. If I leave him in there too long, I'm going to be over here the rest of the season."

The Jayhawks cruised to the Big 12 regular-season title and then smashed in the first-ever conference tournament, beating Oklahoma State by 25, No. 16 Iowa State by 24 and Mizzou by 27 in the title game.

"It was absolutely our mindset that we were going to win the championship," Pollard says, "and finally get Roy his first championship."

The Jayhawks weren't exceptionally sharp the first weekend of the NCAA Tournament — they trailed Purdue in the second round with nine minutes left — but they finished on a 23-8 run to cruise into the Sweet 16.

"We went to Birmingham with a lot of confidence," Robertson says, "but the problem was we were bit by injuries."

In the opener that season against Santa Clara, Haase had fallen on his right wrist. The next day his wrist was so weak that he couldn't pull up his socks. Eventually, however, the pain lessened until midway through the year when he fell on the wrist again, and X-rays showed that it was broken and had been broken. Instead of getting season-ending surgery, Haase toughed it out.

But during that first weekend of the tournament, the pain worsened. It was no longer tolerable, so before KU left for Birmingham, the doctors gave Haase a shot of cortisone.

Turns out, Haase was allergic.

He spent the two nights leading up to the game against Arizona in tears and restless, unable to sleep because of the pain.

"I was actually worried I was gonna get in trouble for breaking curfew because I was walking in the hotel at 2, 3, 4 in the morning," Haase says. "I just couldn't sleep."

On game day during KU's shootaround, Williams asked Haase to shoot a free throw. He airballed it, landing 5 feet short. Haase begged Williams to give him a chance. "Don't make a decision now," he said. "This is all I've ever dreamed about."

"He had tears in his eyes and so did I," Williams says. "And so I said, 'I'm not worried. Let's wait and see.'"

In warmups, Williams asked Haase to take a jumper. It was short but grazed the rim, and he kept Haase in the starting lineup.

"I always wonder and worry to this day," Haase says, "maybe I should have just taken one for the team and not gone out there."

Haase gave his teammates and coaches hope on the opening possession, busting into a passing lane to steal a ball with his left hand and then taking it in for a right-handed finger roll. Pollard stole the ball on the next possession and threw it ahead to Haase, who had a one-on-one against Miles Simon in transition, but he pulled it out and then hesitated when he'd decided to pass to Pierce. His hesitation caused him to travel.

"I remember catching the ball one time, it was in front of their bench and Raef was posting up," Haase recalls. "He was wide open, and all I needed to do was take my right hand, wrap it around, throw it in to him, and I couldn't. I knew I couldn't do it. And so I kept it in my left hand, threw it up top and swung it around. It was just literally playing with one hand and that wasn't going to be good enough to help the team, unfortunately."

In 14 minutes on the floor, Haase did not score again, missed two shots and had three turnovers.

Despite his struggles, KU trailed by only two at halftime. The Jayhawks opened the second half on a 7-2 run, but the game turned when Pollard picked up his third foul on a Michael Dickerson shot. Williams kept Pollard in, and on the next possession, Pollard caught the ball with deep post position against A.J. Bramlett. Pollard power-dribbled before going up, and Bramlett flopped to the floor. The official bought it, calling Pollard's for his fourth foul with 17 minutes left and the score tied at 43.

"I remember cussing at the ref, and he knew he made a bad call," Pollard says. "And he didn't T me up. He probably should have thrown me out of the game for what I said, but I think it was because he knew that he missed that call and he knew that he ended my career, because that's what I told him, and I just walked away.

"That was the hardest part of my whole basketball career was that foul. That was the first time I thought, 'Holy shit, it's my fault. We're not going to win.'"

Without Pollard, the Wildcats took control. Arizona's perimeter trio of Simon, Mike Bibby and Dickerson combined for 58 points.

"Coach always hung his hat on Jacque and Jerod could guard anybody," C.B. McGrath, a junior point guard in '97, says. "Well, they could, but if they can't play, doesn't matter."

Arizona pushed its lead to nine with just under 10 minutes left, and nothing felt right for the Jayhawks with Pollard and Haase on the bench.

"Jerod was our emotional leader," McGrath says. "We fed off his energy because he would make big plays, and he showed it. He showed emotion. Raef sort of played emotionless. Jacque would show emotion here and there. Paul hardly ever showed emotion as a sophomore unless it was frustration. So Jerod's dynamic was very important to our success if things weren't going well."

With 3:28 left, Bibby nailed a 3 that pushed Arizona's lead to 13, and then came the patented Kansas run. Pierce dunked, and Robertson buried a 3. When Billy Thomas hit a 3 with 1:04 left, KU trailed by only three. The two teams started trading 3s for twos from there, with back-to-back Thomas 3s and then a Robertson 3 cutting Arizona's lead to one with 21 seconds left.

The Jayhawks figured it was going to be just like every other game.

"We always thought that we were going to win," McGrath says.

After Bibby made two free throws with 18 seconds left, KU had the ball with a chance to send the game to overtime. Thomas got a good look that went long. The ball was tapped back out to Vaughn, who had space to shoot it, but he passed to a guarded Robertson on the wing. Robertson shot a leaning attempt between two defenders that air-balled. LaFrentz caught it and dribbled to the corner in front of KU's bench, firing off one last guarded attempt at the buzzer.

"Even when Raef took that crappy 3 in the corner, it looked good," Pollard says. "I thought it was gonna go in."

It didn't.

"Arizona has pulled off the biggest upset of this tournament," Jim Nantz shouted on the broadcast.

The dream, their destiny, was over, just like that.

"After that game, I don't know if anybody didn't cry," Pollard says. "I've never seen a whole team crying."

"I have no idea what was said after," Haase says. "I'm sure Coach Williams said some things. I didn't have the capacity to listen or process. Everybody knew what a special team it was, what special year it was. There would be no words that would make it better."

"Not only do we never get to play college basketball again, but we didn't get Roy his goal and what we wanted for ourselves and for the university and for the fans," Pollard says. "We put so much pressure on ourselves to get it for Roy."

It's still hard for them to talk about, an end that's filled with so many what-ifs.

What if Vaughn never falls in the preseason? "He was knocking shots down, and his wrist was never the same," Pollard says. "He didn't even have the same follow-through because his wrist never healed enough to allow him to follow through."

What if Pollard doesn't hurt his foot, or isn't whistled for that fourth foul?

"I was in foul trouble, possibly because I was a step slow because my conditioning wasn't where it should have been," Pollard says. "But maybe not. Maybe it was just because I made bad decisions.

"We knew if we go up against that team 100 more times, we win 99 of them. That's just a fact. We were a much more talented team from top to bottom, and everybody knew that. They caught fire, won six games in a row and won a ring."

And, the one that will forever be debated by KU fans, what if Haase hadn't broken his wrist? Or what if he hadn't played against Arizona? Thomas, who at the time Williams called the best shooter he'd ever coached, was coming off making 3-of-4 3s against Purdue. Against Arizona, the two players who would have played more without Haase — Robertson and Thomas — combined to make seven of KU's 10 3s that day.

"At that time I knew that it might not be best for our team, but there's no way in Hades I was not going to let him have a chance," Williams says. "Looking back on it, I still say it's the stupidest thing I've ever said, but it was true. If you had told me that if by giving him a chance, we were gonna lose the game, I still would have given him the chance."

In the eight years before those seniors arrived on campus, Kansas played in four Final Fours. It was just expected that they'd eventually get there. It almost seemed like a certainty they were going to finish their careers winning a national title.

Williams would get Kansas back to the Final Four five years later. He'd eventually win his first national title in 2005 at North Carolina and win two more before retiring in 2021.

Yet the '96-97 Jayhawks were arguably the best team Williams ever coached. He had built his dream team, and when that group was clicking, it was one of the most dominant the college game has ever seen.

"It was all the things that were right about college basketball," Haase says. "Great coach, great atmosphere, great fans. And to have not capitalized, it hurts to this day." ▬▬

NCAA Tournament 2nd Round

SCORING	1	2	T
Creighton	38	34	72
Kansas	39	40	79

'We're a Different Team with Him'

Behind Remy Martin, Kansas Staves Off Upset Challenge from Creighton

By CJ Moore

MARCH 19, 2022

Remy Martin cannot stop smiling. Four minutes left on the clock inside Dickies Arena in Fort Worth with the game still in doubt, there was Martin smiling as he dribbled up the floor. Afterward, once he'd finished radio responsibilities, Kansas star Ochai Agbaji dapped him up, shouting, "Let's go, boy!" Smiles. At the podium, more smiles.

Martin keeps saying he loves this month and loves playing for this university, and he's like a man who has been given a second chance at life. A few weeks ago Martin being a part of this ride seemed very much in doubt. He was basically put on ice for two months, nursing a bum knee until it felt just right. There were doubts. From Bill Self. From Martin. From his teammates, if they were to be honest.

But Martin's time has finally arrived, and any doubt or frustration is in the past now. Because, by golly, look at Self. He's talking about Martin, and he's smiling too.

"We're a different team with him," Self said after Martin scored a season-high 20 points to help keep the No. 1 seed Jayhawks' season alive with a 79-72 win over ninth-seeded Creighton. Kansas had soundly defeated 16-seed Texas Southern 83-56 in their first game of the tournament.

It was in this round a year before that KU's season ended, and if not for Martin, it may have ended again in the first weekend.

Creighton coach Greg McDermott threw a curveball at the Jayhawks, choosing to guard KU's point guards with his power forward. Check that, guard isn't really the appropriate term here. McDermott

96

chose for his power forward to ignore Kansas' point guards in an effort to clog the paint, taking away driving lanes for Agbaji and Christian Braun and limiting post touches for David McCormack.

The Bluejays called it a personnel game, and they were going to bet that if they slowed Agbaji, Braun and McCormack, forced "the others" to make shots, then maybe an upset was possible. Those others, the logic went, didn't have enough juice.

It didn't necessarily work. Kansas scored a respectable 1.13 points per possession, and Creighton looked foolish for ignoring Martin, who had all the juice. But on the other end, McDermott took another calculated risk. He told his guys to "let it fly," a strategy that also seemed bold considering his team had gone 0 of 20 from 3 in the first halves of the previous two games, but that strategy absolutely had the desired effect. Playing some super-small lineups without star center Ryan Kalkbrenner, who injured his knee ahead of the weekend, McDermott gave his guys the greenest of lights. And it worked wonderfully for him. The basket looked bigger for the Bluejays, and everyone started making 3s — even freshman Arthur Kaluma, who came in shooting just 25 percent from deep.

Kaluma, who was McCormack's matchup when Creighton went small, basically shot the big fella off the floor for a stretch. The Jays buried eight triples in the first half, and Kaluma made two, scoring 13 of his game-high 24 points before halftime. That forced Self to go to his super-small ball lineup, which is one he'd barely played all year.

"It was a hard game for Dave, and Mitch (Lightfoot) isn't quite 100 percent yet," Self said. "So that was a hard matchup."

The beauty of Self's depth, with Martin now in the rotation, is that his roster is like a chameleon. Ideally, Self would have liked to make Creighton adjust to what his team was doing, but it was flipped for a bit. And if the game calls for going small, Self can go there.

Self's preference, however, is to play McCormack, because the big fella is one of the best offensive rebounders in the country and his proficiency for getting to the free-throw line makes him an efficient scorer. This was not McCormack's best game. He scored seven points on eight shots, and KU was outscored by five with him on the floor. And when Kansas needed a bucket down the stretch and tried to exploit his size advantage, he clanked a jump hook off the rim, giving Creighton the ball down one with a chance to take the lead.

The Jays had been like a pack of flies on a hot summer's day, just lingering and waiting for Kansas to break. The Jays finally felt the pressure themselves on the ensuing possession after McCormack's missed jump hook when freshman Trey Alexander threw an errant pass that turned into an Agbaji breakaway dunk. But they were still right there. Down three. Final minute.

Creighton got what appeared to be an advantageous switch when McCormack ended up on Alexander. It's this kind of matchup that Big 12 teams were chasing late in the year. Not only can McCormack struggle in space, but he's playing on a gimpy foot that took some of his giddy-up.

Sometimes McCormack looks like an old man running up and down the floor, but his presence still makes a difference. Creighton, for instance, was just 9-of-31 from inside the arc, and McCormack is the best rim deterrent the Jayhawks have. And maybe he isn't able to chase shooters out on the perimeter for 40 minutes, but with the game on the line, he made the effort in that final minute. He did his job, running Alexander off the 3-point line, but the freshman got his shoulders past and had a path to the basket. The bucket would have cut the lead to one with just over 30 seconds left. Again, the pressure in these situations the later it gets can be too much for a top seed that is expected to win. Kansas has died that death before. Kentucky died that death a day earlier.

But as Alexander headed in to cut the lead to a point and put even more game pressure on KU,

McCormack stayed close enough and finally landed the kill shot on those pesky flies, blocking Alexander's attempt into the glass and into the hands of Martin.

"He didn't ice the game," Self said of McCormack, "but that basically put it out of reach right there."

Martin calmly knocked down the free throws, just as he'd calmly buried those early back-to-back 3s when Creighton left him all alone. Creighton eventually guarded him, and Martin made some late-clock shots when possessions fell apart, and he also took and made some quick shots, a sign that Self is giving him some rope.

"I've said many times in the NCAA Tournament, and it happened with Creighton tonight, you've got to have some guys take some marginal shots and make them," Self said in reference to Martin.

It's not just Self, however, who has given some rope. Martin, too, has met his coach somewhere in the middle. He's come around on buying into all the little things Self wants of him. Let McDermott, who faced Martin two seasons ago when he was at Arizona State, explain.

"His growth and improvement from the guy that was at Arizona State to the guy that's playing now is night and day," McDermott said. "Like his engagement defensively compared to how he defended at Arizona State, and the unselfish nature of the way he's playing is totally different than the guy we played against when he was at Arizona State. So obviously Coach Self and his staff have done a great job of getting him to understand how he can best help this team. And if you look at the stat sheet, there's one thing that jumps out at you today. He was a big difference in this game."

In the last three games, Martin is popping off that stat sheet. He's averaging 15.7 points with an effective field-goal percentage of 62.9, and he has 12 assists and just one turnover. And in two of

those three games, Self has played Martin more than starting point guard Dajuan Harris.

And that takes us back to a year ago, when Self essentially admitted after losing to USC that his roster wasn't good enough. KU needed more athleticism. Needed more scoring and shooting on the perimeter.

It turns out that what Self had was actually pretty good. The core of that team returned. An offseason of work turned those returners into a unit that was good enough to win the toughest league in America and put Kansas on the top line.

But Self was prophetic that to get deeper in the NCAA Tournament, he was going to need another piece. That piece very much kept this run going. And those returners, on this day, were not exactly themselves.

But when and if Agbaji, in a bit of a shooting slump, is Agbaji again, and everything lines up for

the Jayhawks, with Martin enhancing what was already a very good team that made it to the top line, then ...

"I still believe we got another gear," Self said, "or another step we can take."

The Jayhawks will live another day to see if that's true.

This was one of those cliche survive-and-advance days, with Self admitting as much when he was asked if he felt relieved or happy after this win. He answered both, then turned to his players and asked, "How do you guys feel?"

Agbaji: "I'm relieved."

Jalen Wilson: "I'll take the win."

Martin smiled.

On to Chicago, where the journey continues. ▬▬

Remy Martin

How the Jayhawks Point Guard Came Back from an Unsettling Two Months to Keep the Season Alive

By CJ Moore

MARCH 24, 2022

Remy Martin always says the right thing. This season it would have been very easy for Martin to slip. He got off to a good start at Kansas, leading the Jayhawks to a 10-1 record as one of two starting point guards. Then he bumped his knee in a game against Nevada, setting off one of the stranger injury episodes in Kansas basketball history. Martin was in and out of the lineup before eventually sitting for seven straight games. When he finally played, it was in limited circumstances. In the third game back, he played only three minutes. On Senior Day at Allen Fieldhouse two days later, he started but played only seven minutes.

Rumors swirled through the process. Before a mid-January game against West Virginia, it was floated that Martin may not play again. The belief was that the Martin and KU marriage had turned rocky, a rumor that a frustrated coach Bill Self dismissed with an f-bomb.

In the last two weeks, Martin has taken off, showing his coach and his teammates what he was capable of and keeping the Jayhawks' season alive in a game they might have lost without him against Creighton.

And through it all, Martin hasn't slipped. Hasn't said something that could be construed that he was displeased with Kansas. His answers about the process make him sound almost Zen-like. "Control what you can control," he says. "Nobody wants to be around negativity all the time. Energy is contagious."

So polished. So positive. But is it real?

Is Remy Martin full of it?

If you really want to know how Remy Martin feels, just look at his face. It'll tell you. Last weekend in Fort Worth, he was smiling. He couldn't stop. And it was a 180 from where he was a year ago. Those details, the nuance, is all relevant to understand where his mind was this season.

Martin's first three years at Arizona State had him on his way to getting his jersey in the rafters. Arizona State made two straight NCAA Tournaments for the first time since 1981 and was likely on its way to a third when the 2020 season ended prematurely because of COVID-19. On his recruiting visit, he and his dad stood in the middle of the floor at Wells Fargo Arena. The top section of the arena was blocked by removable walls back then, because those seats were often empty. To make the arena not look so empty, they basically shrunk it. "If you come here," Sam Martin told his son, "this building is going to be packed."

Midway through his freshman year, the walls came down, as there was actually a demand for those additional 4,000 seats.

Martin loved a crowd. He's quiet off the floor, but like a Tasmanian devil on it. He's constantly waving his hands to the crowd, imploring everyone to get on their feet and get louder. He's a showman. The louder they got, the better he played.

Without a crowd for his senior season at ASU, the joy just wasn't there. The Sun Devils were ranked 18th in the preseason, because they had Martin and a star-studded freshman class that ranked eighth in the country. They got off to a disappointing 4-3 record, and then Martin's grandfather, Remy Macaspac — whom he was named after — died.

Martin describes his grandpa as the backbone of his family. Macaspac lost his wife, Carmen, in 2003. The couple, who came to the US from the Philippines in 1972, had seven children. And every Sunday after Carmen's death, Grandpa Remy, his seven children and their families would meet at Forrest Lawn Cemetery, share memories and then a picnic meal. Afterward, they would go to someone's house and hang out. They were all constantly together.

Martin idolized his grandpa, who was a handyman and built him his first basketball court. His family hadn't alerted him that the end was near because they didn't want to distract him from basketball, and the loss hit him hard.

Martin missed two games to go back home for his grandpa's funeral — both losses. As the season progressed, it became apparent he wasn't himself. Add up everything — the loss of his grandpa, losing games, no longer playing in front of packed arenas — and it just wasn't fun anymore.

"He didn't smile much at all," Sam says. "It wasn't a good year. It wasn't a productive year. It wasn't about team. It was a lot of individualism on that team. Everybody's trying to get theirs. Everybody's trying to go to the next level and not understanding that if you win, it helps us all go to the next level."

During the recruitment process, Sam had also told his son that Arizona State was a place that would allow Remy to be Remy. "Anywhere else you go, they're going to mold you to play their game," he said at the time. "This place will let you be you."

"It played out maybe too good," Sam says now. "Because it let him be himself too much. And sometimes, sometimes Remy needs to be saved from Remy."

The need for a change smacked Sam in the face late in the year on what was Martin's original Senior Day against Washington State. Martin missed 10 of his first 11 3-point attempts that day, and after one of those misses, the ASU fans booed.

"Instead of saying, 'Remy, listen, hold the reins. Stop taking those shots. They're not falling. Let's do something different,' Remy continued to shoot them," Sam says. "He doesn't listen to the crowd."

After nine straight misses, Martin finally made a 3. Then with the game tied at 74 in overtime and the clock ticking toward zero, he pulled up eight feet behind the line and buried the game-winner. What allowed him to make that shot was his short-term memory. "He doesn't remember what happened yesterday," his dad says. But the end result did not change what his father believed he needed.

With an extra year of eligibility possible, Martin decided if he didn't stay in the NBA Draft that he was going to spend his super senior season somewhere other than Arizona State.

Kansas had recruited Martin out of high school, and the memory of playing at Allen Fieldhouse as a Sun Devils freshman had never left him. He knew the place was different when he saw fans lined up outside hours before the game. "This place must be amazing," he remembers thinking. He says he was so worked up when he got in the game that he air-balled his first shot. That was over five years ago, so worth a fact check. His memory is spot on. His first shot sailed over the rim. He scored 21 points that day as Arizona State pulled off the 95-85 upset. It was a performance that Self also never forgot.

When Martin hit the transfer portal, Self called around and came away convinced that Martin was the missing piece that could get his team to a Final Four.

Martin knew what he wanted out of it: "A national championship," he says. "Simple as that."

And his father was confident Kansas was the best spot for his son.

"Because Coach Self," Sam says. "Coach Self is going to hold you accountable. Coach Self is going to make sure you play as a team."

Coming to KU was a chance to change the narrative.

"People have short-term memories as well," Sam says.

Both Martin and his father believe he'd been mislabeled as a score-first point guard. He turned into that at Arizona State out of necessity — averaging 19.1 points per game in each of his final two seasons in Tempe — but he'd grown up as more of a facilitator and never the first option. His father believes Martin's best year at Arizona State was his sophomore season when he averaged only 12.9 points but a career-best 5.0 assists. The next two seasons when Martin had to score more, it changed how he played in a negative way.

"He wasn't defending the way he used to defend because he's trying to save energy for offense," Sam says. "So he had to conserve energy on the defensive end and he maybe wasn't being held accountable as much as he should be."

Martin didn't want to be the guy anymore. He wanted to play the game in "its purest form," meaning an unselfish style where the ball finds the open man and no one cares who scores. He also wanted teammates he knew could get the job done.

"As a player, sometimes you know that a team has an advantage on you," he says. "And coming to Kansas, it's like we have the advantage every time. At every position we're pretty strong."

He pauses.

"I had the greatest four years of my life there," he says. "Just here was a better shot for me."

The transition was not exactly seamless, because Martin had a lot of old habits Self was going to break. Nothing was going to be overlooked. It was an entirely new reality for the point guard.

"If I made a mistake in a game, he would take me out. I'm not very used to being taken out the game so early," Martin says. "He'd tell me those mistakes can't happen, especially where we're trying to get to. He made sure I was aware that those things could cost us the season or the game. Made me understand you can't take any possessions off.

Every possession counts, and I think at ASU I kind of forgot about that."

Self has the ability to watch the game as if a microscope is locked on every player. Martin admits he had a bad habit of taking his time getting to a spot on the floor, because at Arizona State, it didn't really matter where he went; he was always coming back to the ball eventually. That didn't fly at Kansas. Every movement matters and must be done with purpose. Defensively, Martin wasn't always in tune with where he needed to be off the ball. Self wouldn't let any of it slip. And when he got on Martin, it didn't bother him. He understood it. He embraced it.

When Martin didn't start the first exhibition game because he hadn't aced some of those details yet, he didn't pout. He kept trying to get better. And his start to the season was pretty good. The Jayhawks had the third-best offense in college basketball with a healthy Martin. Some games he would score. Some games he'd distribute.

"(Christian Braun) and (Ochai Agbaji) were really taking off at the time, "Martin says. "I was just getting them the ball, and winning was the most important thing. That's why I came here. So it just felt normal just playing and, you know, making the right play and not having to shoot too much. I was just making sure my guys were good. That's what I came here to do."

And then, the knee injury …

It was diagnosed as a bone bruise, which doesn't sound that bad, but the pain was like nothing Martin had experienced before.

"I couldn't bend my knee," he says. "I would get on a bike and I wouldn't even be able to get over the bike. It was hard for me to walk. It just hurt. And then when it got better, I'd hurt it again in practice and it was setback after setback."

Nothing structurally was wrong with Martin's knee, so that's where it became difficult to know when the right time was to return. He initially sat one game, then started the next and played 25 minutes in a win at Oklahoma State. Then he came off the bench the next game and played only 12 minutes. He sat out the next two games, then played the next four. He didn't look right, averaging only 3.3 points in 17.8 minutes per game during that stretch, which led to a decision to sit until he felt right.

This is where it got … complicated.

"He's a pretty quiet kid," Self says. "If he's got an issue, in many ways, he just feels like, 'Well, I can handle that on my own.' Through his injury, I felt like I never knew exactly where he was."

That made it difficult for Self to communicate Martin's status to the outside world. There were several times during his seven-game absence when Martin would practice the day before a game and then on game day say he couldn't play. And anytime Self would ask how he was feeling, he'd say he was feeling better.

"He didn't want to come off as being not as tough by saying I can't go," Self says.

Kurtis Townsend, who recruited Martin in high school, would touch base with Martin often, and the messaging from Martin, again, was always positive. So much so that even Townsend began to question what was going on.

"To be honest, at first I was like, 'God dang. Is this kid full of crap or is he always like this?' You know what I mean?" Townsend says. "I was like, it's just too good. He always says the right stuff. And you know how you could be fooled by people? But when I talk to his teammates, they go, 'No, Coach, that's how he is every day.' He's a really good teammate."

The uncertainty created speculation that something bad was going on behind the scenes.

"One-hundred percent false," Sam says. "Just a bad rumor."

When Martin did return, he was eased back in, and the lack of playing time created even more speculation.

"He wasn't quite ready to play," Self says. "But the bottom line is he also had not been out there playing with his teammates enough to probably look good until he kind of got comfortable again, and that took a couple of weeks in itself."

Throughout the process, Sam kept telling his son a line he's given him since he was a child: "Don't get bitter. Get better."

The time finally came at the Big 12 tournament. Martin was starting to look like himself again, so Self gave him a chance. Martin played well in wins over TCU and Texas Tech, scoring 22 points and dishing seven assists in the two games to help KU win the tournament.

Then in the opening weekend of the NCAA Tournament, he was the star. Agbaji, the Jayhawks' All-American, was off, but Martin picked up the slack and was electric. His burst was back. He was scoring. He was distributing.

Watching him, Townsend says it's a shame the injury happened because KU's record would be even better had that guy been present all season.

"Reality of it is," Self says now with the benefit of hindsight, "he knew his body better than anybody else. He could have gone, but he would have been at 75 percent, and 75 percent when you have to deal with explosiveness isn't enough. It was a little frustrating — for him and for us. But he handled it right. I got to give it to him. He handled it right."

Self's mind is racing, and he's going through all the ways his players can adjust to Martin now and how he's begun to tinker. "I'm being too detailed,"

he says, realizing he's giving away some of his trade secrets, bottom-lining it like this: "That's why I think we can get better. I think we're getting more used to playing with him."

It would have been easy during that teeter-tottering two-plus months for Martin to feel like an outsider. He says he never did, but it's only human nature to feel that, right? After Kansas beat Texas Southern in the first round, Martin sat at the podium with Self, Braun and point guard Dajuan Harris. His teammates were asked what he brings to the team. Both Harris and Braun said nice things, and Martin sat there smiling, and then mouthed, "Thanks, guys."

He's loving every second of this, and he has perspective, too. Listen to what he says, and it's hard to believe there was ever bitterness toward his coach.

"He's been awesome, and I always will respect him and love him for the way he's handled me," Martin says of Self. "He helped me with my game and my life. He's taught me a lot. And I think he kind of brought that dog out of me again."

Self has always been good at the psychology of the game, knowing what buttons to push. Martin is a little tougher to gauge, because "he's a lively dude on the floor and really laid back off of it," Self says.

But what Self is learning is that the bigger the stage, the better Martin plays.

Townsend, who has been with Self since 2004, noticed last week that Self is giving the point guard more rope now. "Because he knows that he is trying to do what we want him to defensively," Townsend says.

The other part of it is, by leaving him out there, Self knows the reward is eventually coming.

The Jayhawks also had hit a bit of rut late in the year, and they needed a jolt. "His energy's been fantastic," Self says. "It's contagious. This team needed some personality, and I think he's helped provide that."

The one thing that's been missing during Martin's second turn at a senior season is his crowd. At Arizona State, he often had a lot of family in the stands. He's always been used to being around them. The biggest crowd he ever had was a home game against Arizona his junior season when he scored 24 points. At the time, it was his third win in the previous four tries against Arizona and he'd averaged 24.8 points in those games. Sam says they nicknamed him the "Cat Killer."

After winning the Big 12 tournament, Martin returned to the floor afterward, and the only one there to see him was his girlfriend, who drove up from Dallas. His dad was there in Fort Worth. A few more family members are making the trip to Chicago. And if Kansas wins two more games?

"It might look like the Philippines if they make the Final Four," Sam says.

Martin likes to say everything has come full circle for him this year. He started his career as a sixth man, bringing energy off the bench. He's ending it as a sixth man in a similar role.

Most players care about starting, but this is yet another example of Martin saying the right thing. But does he mean it?

The longer you listen, the more you start to believe maybe it is sincere. Remy Martin is not full of it.

His Kansas experience has not been ideal, but his reason for coming is still right there and you better believe he's ready for it.

"Remy loves the moment," his dad says. "He loves this shit. He wants the moment. He wants to be the guy that took that last down by two with 10 seconds left. He thrives on that. He runs to it. He doesn't run from it." ▬▬▬

NCAA Tournament Sweet 16

```
SCORING        1   2   T
Providence    17  44  61
Kansas        26  40  66
```

Play Hard, Play Ugly

Kansas Following a Familiar Script to Keep Advancing in NCAA Tournament

By CJ Moore

MARCH 25, 2022

Bill Self did the sideline shuffle when he saw Providence was in a zone for the second straight possession out of the final media timeoutt. Self had been waiting for the Friars to go zone all game. Providence had scouted Kansas as well as anyone. With nearly a week to prepare for the Sweet 16, the Providence players knew KU's playbook almost as well as the Jayhawks know it.

You could say the same on the other end. The game looked ugly, yes, but it had a lot to do with each team's preparation and attention to detail on the defensive end. Add the officials allowing a wee bit of contact, and this was like two teams trying to hoop in the mud.

The trap a lot of coaches fall in during games like this one is just putting the ball in your star's hands in the final minutes and hoping he makes a play. It's like the playbook goes in the dumpster. But Self had an inkling that Ed Cooley would employ his zone coming out of the timeout, and Self decided to add a little beauty to this trudge match.

He screamed the call to his team, pulling the lever to launch his star before Providence's coaches could react. Ochai Agbaji, put in a straitjacket all night, clapped for the ball from his spot in the corner — a deceptive move to distract from what was coming. When Remy Martin swung the ball to Christian Braun, Providence's Justin Minaya, standing right next to Agbaji, relaxed for a split second. That's all it took. Agbaji ran behind him, David McCormack took out the middle man in the zone, Braun threw the ball to the corner of the backboard just like he's taught and Agbaji threw down the knockout blow.

Kansas 66, Providence 61.

"That guy's in the Hall of Fame for a reason," Cooley said. "Agbaji's a top-five player in America for a reason. You're not going to stop everything they do."

Providence certainly tried, hanging around long enough that what felt like an inevitable Kansas win for most of the night nearly turned into a nightmare finish. Instead, the Jayhawks kept their dream alive, into the Elite Eight without really playing a great game yet in this tournament. Agbaji, their All-American, is averaging 10.3 points and shooting 33.3 percent from the field the last three games.

Every game follows the same pattern. Both teams feel each other out early, then Self unleashes his Microwave Man off the bench, and Martin cooks to give Kansas the lead. Martin scored seven points in his first 90 seconds on the floor, giving KU a nice seven-point cushion early.

Self has been talking a lot lately to his team about making sure the other team plays bad. You don't have to make shots when you pull that off, and Kansas put together one of its most dominant defensive halves of the season in the first 20 minutes. Kansas had just as many blocks (seven) in the first half as Providence's baskets.

All year the Jayhawks have employed a switching scheme off the ball where they switch every action. They weren't always connected, but they're there now. The Jayhawks could have told you the Providence pregame meal during those first 20 minutes, right down to who had onions. It wasn't just tough for the Friars to make a shot. Hell, it was tough to get enough space to shoot a brick.

Cooley, to his credit, found something in the second half with Al Durham working out of middle ball screens. The Friars, after scoring only 17 first-half points, put up 44 in the second half.

But that Self fella, the Hall of Famer, also knew what button to push.

In a tournament where the vulnerabilities of the top seeds have sent them home early, Kansas is the one with the most counter punches. Jalen Wilson, Braun and Agbaji are the best wing trio in the country, and they have all taken their turns this season attacking whoever the opposing weak link is. The ball keeps swinging until they find their guy, and on this night it was Wilson's advantage. It wasn't his best game — 16 points on 16 shots — but he did enough to keep the season alive, attacking the Providence target: forward Noah Horchler.

"If we move the ball and I'm able to get a closeout from the slot, it's kind of hard to guard, especially with how fast we're moving out there," Wilson said. "I just took advantage."

Not a lot else worked. Not post-ups for David McCormack or Mitch Lightfoot. Not pin downs for Agbaji. As Self has said through this tourney run, it's hard to run plays in this setting. It's all about players making plays.

That's why Martin has been the savior. He seems to thrive in chaos. At one point on Friday when Self was screaming at Lightfoot for not executing a set correctly, a split-second later Martin hit Lightfoot with a no-look dart for a dunk.

It's not just his scoring, either. That's nice, of course, because he dropped 23 in this one. But Martin in place of Dajuan Harris is opening up wider lanes for those slot drives for Wilson and Braun. At some point, you'd think, the shots are going to fall and it'll be the Kansas offense that just overwhelms an opponent in this tournament.

What's happened so far is a lot like the 2012 run, when Kansas labored through the second and third games and then put together a performance easy on the eyes against North Carolina to get to the Final Four.

Maybe that's coming up against Miami.

This game against Providence, like Creighton, will go in the thankful-to-survive-and-advance category, no apology forthcoming.

"When it's ugly and it comes to defense and rebounding and playing like that," Wilson said, "if we went like that every game, I'm not really tripping."

The Jayhawks aren't strutting into the Elite Eight, but maybe they should be. They are the favorites in this tournament now. Their defense is better than ever. They now have the best sixth man in America. They have the only first-team All-American left in the field.

And when it comes time to win late, the Jayhawks have to feel good about having Martin to improvise and Self at the controls. Against the team considered "luckiest" in college basketball for its ability to win close games, Self knew the way to stomp on that four-leaf clover: Throw that thing up for Agbaji.

"Sometimes when you're really struggling and you got a guy that go upstairs like that," Self said. "Sometimes, that's the easiest basket you can get." ▬▬

NCAA Tournament Elite Eight

SCORING	1	2	T
Miami	35	15	50
Kansas	29	47	76

'Do the Little Things Right'

Bill Self, Kansas Put It All Together Against Miami to Reach Final Four

By CJ Moore

MARCH 27, 2022

single tear welled up in the corner of his left eye as a celebration went on around him, and Bill Self thought about his father. "I talked to him more today," Self said, "than I have in a while."

His father, Bill Self Sr., gave his son the coaching gene and taught him a valuable life lesson that he's always applied to his profession. Don't blow up about the big things, but sweat the small stuff. The day after he lost his dad in late January, his heart still hurting, Self heard Bill Sr.'s voice in his ear when his team trailed by 16 on the road against rival Kansas State, and he remained calm.

We got to do the little things right, he told his players at halftime that day.

The Jayhawks won, of course, and it's one of those moments that will always stay with the coach. They were already special, but giving him that gift has reserved them a unique place in his heart. Self has watched this group grow up the last two years, from one of his worst teams a season ago to winning a share of the Big 12 and winning the conference tourney and then finding themselves on the doorstep of the Final Four. He wanted so badly for them to have their March moment for so many reasons. They'd almost wanted it too much, scratching and clawing their way to the Elite Eight despite never really playing their game.

In the first 20 minutes against Miami, it was clear to everyone in attendance what was going on.

"They were tight," Olofu Agbaji, father of All-American Ochai Agbaji, said.

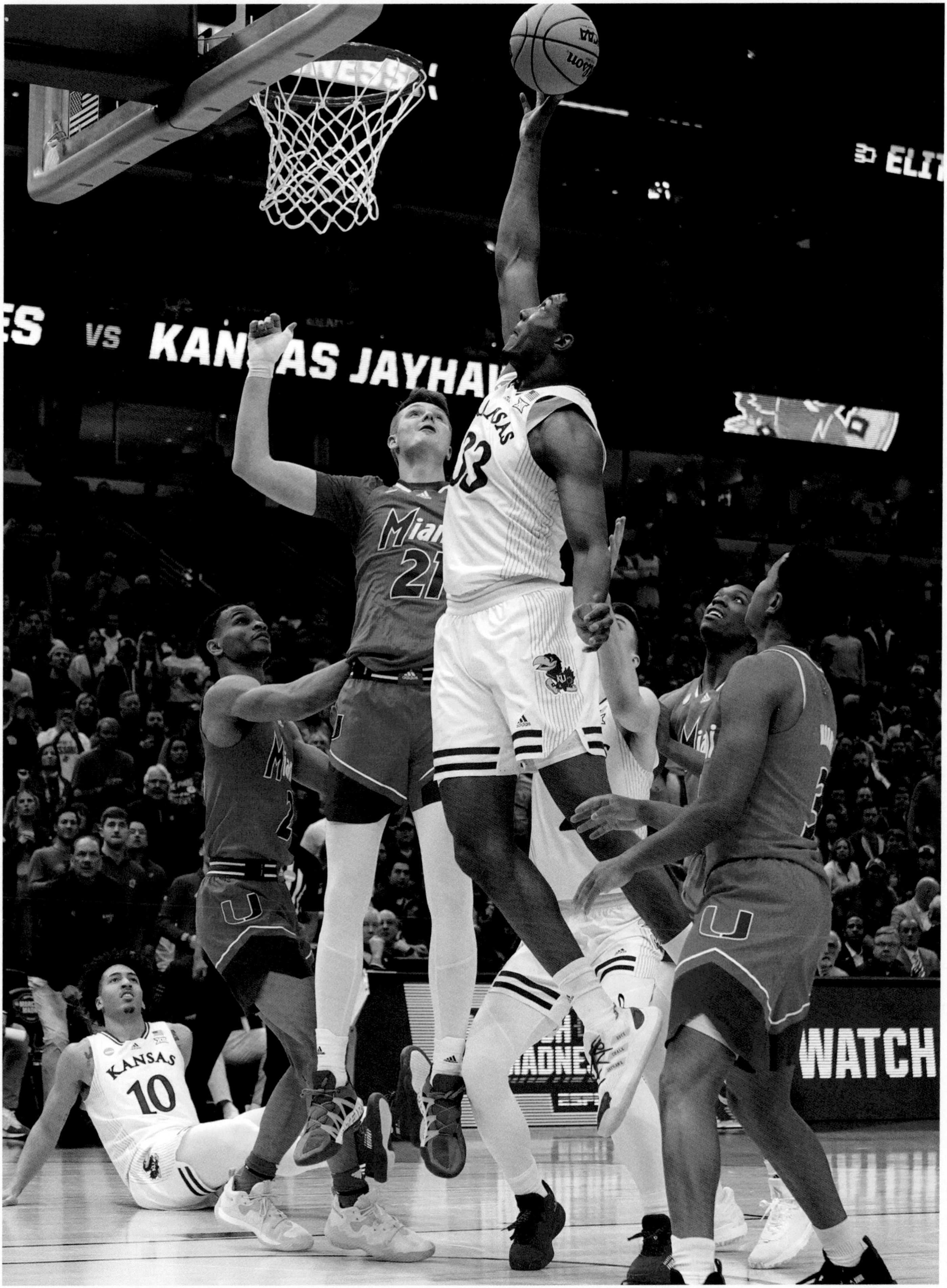
VS
KANSAS
10
21
WATCH

"He's got to pull the trigger," Lisa Braun said of her son, Christian Braun, who turned down multiple 3-point looks.

"He needs to play loose and have confidence," she said to her family. "He'll do it later on. He'll do it."

It wasn't just that the Jayhawks were playing with a belly of nerves the first 20 minutes that had Self in a mood, it was the small details they weren't executing. Jumping at pump fakes. Switching too much. Playing on their heels. "No energy!" Self yelled at his team early after a poor defensive sequence.

"I was very positively pissed," he'd say after.

In that moment, Self found himself looking upward. "Hey dad, we're here. What do you think?"

Dad wasn't keeping him calm this time. Miami led by six at the break. Self's halftime speech will forever stay in the locker room — or until time ultimately loosens lips — but most of it, one can assume, was not fit for a family audience. "We did not come this far to lay down," was the gist of it, Agbaji did allow. Once Self let them have it, he got back to those small details.

The Jayhawks had been provided a smart game plan. Instead of cross-matching position for position, Self had decided to move center David McCormack onto power forward Jordan Miller. Sam Waardenburg, Miami's center who sets most of the ball screens, is an elite pick-and-pop weapon. McCormack has struggled to guard such actions all season, so Self made sure Miami didn't have that option. Waardenburg scored only five points in the first half and made just one 3.

But the Hurricanes came with their own strategic attack, spending the first half trying to get Jalen Wilson switched onto guard Kameron McGusty and letting him go to work. McGusty scored 18 points before the break, but his half finished with KU freshman KJ Adams locking him up on the final possession, leaving him stuck in the air

without a plan right before the buzzer. Self told his team that was the best 29 seconds anyone had played the first half and challenged the regulars to guard as Adams had. He told starting point guard Dajuan Harris that he had McGusty, and he was to face-guard him and not switch. (McGusty scored only four points after halftime.) The Jayhawks would also stick with their original game plan of continuing to feed the ball to the post, a clear weakness for Miami that the KU coaches could see on film.

In the final moments of halftime, Kansas players huddled around their coach for their final marching orders, and Miami had no such huddle. The Hurricanes' starting five strolled onto the floor as chill as if they were about to take on the next five during a Sunday run at the Y.

In the Kansas locker room during this late-season run, they've had a rallying cry: Make them play bad.

Assistant coach Jeremy Case reminded Agbaji of that before he took the floor and said the game would be won with defense and in transition. These Jayhawks have always been better when playing with pace.

That was one of the changes from a year ago. This same core, minus Remy Martin, was not a good transition team. Martin, like a shot of Red Bull, brought that from the very beginning. During a scrimmage in KU's youth camp in the summer, he got paired with Agbaji. It was the first time the eventual roommates had ever played together. All Agbaji had seen before that was this soft-spoken guy. Then Martin got on the floor and started buzzing.

"It was like, 'Who is this?' He's over here screaming in front of the campers, running around," Agbaji said. "It was like a complete 180."

Agbaji, who was freshly back from his NBA Draft experience, remembers Martin instilling a confidence in him to shoot his shot. "He kind of

spread it to everyone else," Agbaji said. "That is something that was missing —just that swagger. CB had it in some spurts. I had in some spurts. But it wasn't like fully there."

Even in his absence, when Martin was sidelined and not really a regular for two-and-a-half months, he had given the Jayhawks that gift.

When the second half started, the Hurricanes tried to use Self's pregame adjustment against Kansas, running an isolation play for Miller. It resulted in a turnover. Then on KU's first possession, Agbaji fed McCormack in the post and he was fouled. The Jayhawks kept feeding McCormack, and he scored the first five second-half points. McCormack's baskets allowed the Jayhawks to collectively breathe again.

After the big fella's spurt, Agbaji got an and-one layup, then Wilson made an acrobatic layup — tossing it in over his head and Waardenburg's reach — and then Braun got a runout dunk to tie

the game. In the first four minutes, Kansas had checked all those halftime boxes except for one. It was time for a certain someone to shoot his shot.

Braun has broken out this year by showing his athleticism and attacking the rim, but Self has continued to tell him that he needs to shoot more. He turns down too many 3s, the coach says, and his hesitancy to pull the trigger in the first half spread like a disease. "Everybody tells me that, it's not just Coach," Braun said. "When I'm open, shoot it."

On the possession after his dunk, when Agbaji dribbled to the right wing in front of KU's bench and handed it off to Braun, he listened to those voices in his ear. This time he pulled the trigger from deeeep, a 3 finally falling in after the Jayhawks had missed their first six.

Miami called timeout, Braun screamed toward the Kansas cheering section in the United Center and then turned and punched the air. It was as if he had been handed the needle to pop Miami's balloon. The Jayhawks had the lead, and with that mountain of pressure off their backs, they had their swag back.

From there, they kept making the Canes play bad, outscoring Miami 47-15 in the second half on their way to a 76-50 win.

Before the starters would spend the final minutes watching from their bench, Agbaji would get the cleanest look he's had this NCAA Tournament in the left corner on a wild sequence that saw him miss a layup, Wilson chase it down, then pitch it out to him. After Agbaji made it, he turned to the crowd, made an X with his arms and yelled "it's over" as he made the universal signal like an umpire calling safe.

It was the most un-Agbaji move ever. When asked afterward if he'd ever seen his son do anything like that, Agbaji's father laughed and said no. "At this stage," he said, "he's entitled to do whatever he wants, especially after the last game was really tough for him. I'm happy to see the ball go through the basket."

Those two second-half 3s were only his third and fourth in this tournament after making 92 in the first 33 games. He'd played like an All-American defensively throughout the tourney, but on this day — scoring 18 points — he looked the part again on both ends.

When the Jayhawks took the stage to celebrate, it was Agbaji's roommate Martin who was announced as the region's Most Outstanding Player, the first time this year that someone other than Agbaji had won such an award for Kansas. The Jayhawks would have never wanted Agbaji to go cold, but in retrospect, it may not have been the worst thing for them to see they could win without his scoring. This team wasn't built to be the Ochai Agbaji Show. The plan, especially after landing Martin, was that KU would have five guys who could go off on any night. As they head to New Orleans, that second half was the vision playing out in its best form.

Self watched it unfold with pride in his heart, knowing where this group once was.

"People don't realize that the group that won a national championship lost in the first round and struggled, and then they finally got there," he said. "Last year's group wasn't ready. This year's group was more prepared just because of maturity and age."

The tear in his eye had finally fallen, running down the side of his nose.

His son, Tyler Self, says this season has been as emotionally exhausting as any he can remember for his dad. He didn't have to say why. There's the NCAA investigation dragging on, Martin's long absence with a knee injury and the loss of his father. Then on after Kansas beat Providence in the Sweet 16, Self's mother, Margaret, fell and hit her head on a marble floor and spent the night in the hospital. Margaret Self made it to the game against Miami, and came down the stairs immediately after to meet her son for a celebratory embrace and kiss.

He's on his way to his fourth Final Four, and the first one without his father. But, somewhere, his dad's watching. Helping him lead and focus on the little things. ▰▰▰

The Avengers

Kansas Earns Final Four Trip Two Years After the Great What-If

By Brian Hamilton

MARCH 29, 2022

After the confetti settled on the midcourt logo and the trophy presentation dais disappeared into the back, but shortly before the hilariously aggressive United Center security chief barked that he was five minutes away from kicking everyone out, Donny Braun stood at the apex of a 3-point line facing a rim with no net. His son's team was headed to the Final Four. Some family picture-taking awaited him. But first, the father of Jayhawks star Christian Braun stretched his arms out wide. He lifted his head and looked to the ceiling.

It was precisely 4:35 p.m. Central Daylight Time on March 27, 2022: the moment he'd been waiting for, as it turned out.

"I knew someday I would get here," Donny announced, to everyone and no one in particular. "I knew someday I would get here."

The story, of course, was not the understandable indulgence of a happy dad. Players and coaches leading the program to just its second national semifinal in a decade: kind of a bigger deal. Still, the sentiment was fair and indicative enough, because the wait arguably shouldn't have been this long. The wait, really, shouldn't have existed in the first place. On this day, a top-seeded Kansas team that's a verified national title contender earned a spot on the final weekend of this event. It was the first part of the answer to one of the bigger what-ifs in program history. It was a scene more than a few people in Chicago thought would have played out somewhere else two years ago.

Someday, and whatever longing comes with it, never should've entered the chat.

Kansas was in the fateful position of being the best team in the country in March of 2020. An almost certainly top-seeded, verified national title contender. A strong favorite to create many photo ops for friends and family alike. And then, well, you know. And now one unforgettable moment gives a team

purpose to create another one, entirely and cathartically different from the first. "This year," center David McCormack said, "feels like we're avenging that year."

That year, to review, featured 28 wins in 31 tries. One loss in the Big 12 regular season. Five weeks spent as the No. 1 team in the Associated Press poll and only one week spent outside of the top 5 … at No. 6. The No. 1 spot atop the KenPom. com ratings at season's end. A roster featuring a conference player of the year who was also maybe the best defensive frontcourt player in the country, a wing who was the conference defensive player of the year and probably the best wing defender in the country, and a leading scorer who was a consensus second-team All-American. A clinical offense and an insatiate defense. It did not require much imagination, if any, to envision the group delivering national championship No. 2 to its head coach.

Eight members of this Kansas team were part of that Kansas team, one way or another. Outside of a sophomore named Ochai Agbaji ending the season as the 2019-20 team's third-leading scorer, they weren't the core drivers of that success. They nevertheless knew quite well what they were missing when everything was taken away by an invisible, invasive hand. "That would've been a championship, too," now-redshirt sophomore Jalen Wilson said. "That was the best team in the nation."

Here we can acknowledge there are more important things than playing a basketball tournament. We also can acknowledge, fairly, the significance of playing in that basketball tournament for the participants, particularly the ones who are really good at basketball. So the reactions to a potential championship run preempted by a pandemic were about as visceral as you'd expect.

"Devastated," Wilson said.

"A heartbreak feeling," McCormack said.

"For it to get canceled like that," Christian Braun said, "kind of sucked for a while."

How long anyone dwelled on it, especially considering the circumstances the world found itself in, probably depends on who you ask. The uneven, disappointing 2020-21 season that followed surely didn't help the mental recovery process. (Though it threw some dry logs on a simmering fire in its own way.) And this Kansas group isn't that Kansas group. There's high-end talent but not as much, the offense is about three points per 100 possessions better, these Jayhawks play faster, and the defense is not as terrifying. As Bill Self put it succinctly in Chicago: "I never felt like this team was the best team in the country this year."

But it's a very good team. And for a very good team, some carryover memories about a very great team can be extremely useful. "Having different leaders, not having just one guy that can do it all — we have plenty of guys who can do everything," Wilson said. "People guard Ochai so hard, it's hard for him to go score 20. We all have to step up. And that team had a lot of different guys that could."

"Just how confident we are in our approach to all the games kind of relates back to that 2020 team," Agbaji said. "Everyone's same vision on that 2020 team was a national championship. And everyone's this year has been a national championship from the second we started the season."

Maybe, deep down in places he doesn't talk about at parties, the sting hasn't abated for the head coach. Self has 761 career wins and counting, the sort of stack you point at, saying nothing, when anyone wonders how much you've accomplished. And yet. There's a lot of meaningful space between a first championship and a next championship. When you know you have the best shot, and you've been around long enough to know how rare it is to have the best shot, and you don't even get a chance to take your best shot, it must be vexing, to put it politely.

Or it could be that this Kansas team has given its coach just enough justification to flick away any remaining what-ifs.

"I don't really think about it a lot," Self said of 2020. "I hear a lot of people talk about, well, we would have been a high seed or a 1 seed or we had a great chance to go deep in the tournament. And that's true. But that team was different. There's not very many teams you could ever put out there that would be the national defensive player of the year is your center and the national defensive player of the year is your guard. I mean, that team could really guard. That was a different level defensive team. This year's team is different, totally. But I do think that this year's team has the same chance to do as well just because they have a strong belief that they can accomplish anything. And it's been impressive for me to watch them grow in that belief this year."

And so Kansas is on to New Orleans, that city of sweaty mysticism and a fine place to complete an exorcism.

Though it's also possible the Jayhawks' spirits are cleansed before arrival. The day before the team secured its spot in the final weekend — many hours before someday arrived — Agbaji sat at a table inside the United Center Concert Club, a snazzy space for pregame or pre-event merriment turned into an ad hoc Midwest Region interview room. The cameras fixed on the now-senior All-American, and the recording devices recorded. He and Kansas were one win away from a Final Four. He and Kansas were on the verge of doing something they figured would be long done by now.

So he was asked: If he ever considers what could have been, what does it look like?

"This," Ochai Agbaji said. "This is what we envisioned." ▬▬

This book is available in quantity at special discounts for your group or organization.
For further information, contact:

Triumph Books LLC
814 North Franklin Street
Chicago, Illinois 60610
Phone: (312) 337-0747
www.triumphbooks.com

Printed in U.S.A.
ISBN: 978-1-63727-141-4

The Athletic

Paul Fichtenbaum, Chief Content Officer
Dan Kaufman, Editorial Director
Lisa Wilson, Editorial Director
Evan Parker, SVP/GM Content Operations
Hugh Kellenberger, Senior Managing Editor - College Basketball
Oscar Murillo, VP Design
Wes McCabe, Design Director
Kenny Dorset, Social Engagement
Trevor Gibbons, Partnerships Director
Jenna Winchell, Marketing Director
Casey Malone, Associate CRM Director
Amanda Ephrom, Brand Strategist
Tyler Sutton, Marketing Manager
Martin Oppegaard, Programming Manager
Ankur Chawla, Business Development
Brooks Varni, Editorial Operations

Featured writers from The Athletic
Eamonn Brennan, Brian Hamilton, CJ Moore, Dana O'Neil, Brendan Quinn

Special thanks to the entire The Athletic College Basketball Staff

Content packaged by Mojo Media, Inc.
Joe Funk: Editor
Jason Hinman: Creative Director

Unless otherwise noted, all interior photos by AP Images